THE POLITICS OF WRITING IN THE TWO-YEAR COLLEGE

Edited by
Barry Alford
and
Keith Kroll

CHARLES I. SCHUSTER, SERIES EDITOR

Boynton/Cook Publishers
HEINEMANN
Portsmouth, NH

Boynton/Cook Publishers, Inc.
A subsidiary of Reed Elsevier Inc.
361 Hanover Street
Portsmouth, NH 03801–3912
www.boyntoncook.com

Offices and agents throughout the world

Library of Congress Cataloging-in-Publication Data
The politics of writing in the two-year college / edited by Barry Alford and Keith Kroll.
    p.   cm.—(CrossCurrents)
    Includes bibliographical references.
    ISBN 0-86709-505-9 (alk. paper)
    1. English language—Rhetoric—Study and teaching—Political aspects—United States.
    2. Report writing—Study and teaching (Higher)—Political aspects—United States.
    3. Community colleges—Curricula.   4. Junior colleges—Curricula.   5. College teachers.
    Part-time.   I. Alford, Barry.   II. Kroll, Keith,   III. CrossCurrents (Portsmouth, NH).

    PE1405.U6 P65 2001
    808′.071′173—dc21

                                    00-051923

Series editor: Charles I. Schuster
Editor: Lisa Luedeke
Production service: Denise Botelho, Colophon
Production coordinator: Elizabeth Valway
Cover design: Joni Doherty Design
Manufacturing: Louise Richardson

Printed in the United States of America on acid-free paper
05 04 03 02 01 VP 1 2 3 4 5

Contents

Acknowledgments

Putting this collection of essays together has been a long and unpredictable journey. We thank the contributors for their patience and perseverance over the years that it took to bring this volume to fruition.

We also thank Chuck Schuster who provided a patient and guiding influence over the project and stuck with it, and us, over the long haul. Ira Shor, who was generous enough to provide the Afterword to the collection, also supplied early suggestions, readings, and insights. In a larger sense, his work is the starting point for much of the critical work done in and on the two-year colleges, and if we do justice to this influence this collection will be a success.

We thank Sylvia Conway and Kim Barnes, who provided invaluable technical support.

Finally, we thank our families for putting up with us during this project, and we also thank the host of community-college colleagues, especially Jim VanderMey and Lucia Elden, who provide us with the examples of oppositional and wise practice that continue to make the two-year college a place we are proud to call home.

Introduction

These essays mean everything. These essays mean nothing.

They mean everything because they bring the voices of practitioners too often silent in the debate over literacy practices, training, and assessment to bear in ways that challenge universalized concepts of what the writing requirement stands for. They mean nothing because two-year college faculty seldom benefit from the effort to publish. The contributors to this volume have, for the most part, wrangled the time to write out of the customary five-course-per-semester load facing most two-year college faculty. Their reward is not part of a tenure-and-promotion package but an active voice in the practices and assumptions affecting their classrooms and their students.

Although the number of students enrolled in writing classes in the two-year colleges has increased, reaching 1.3 million in 1991 (Cohen & Ignash 1992, 54), the frequency of two-year college faculty publishing or presenting at national conferences declined from 1989 to 1991. The disparity between the growth of student enrollment and the decline of active faculty participation in the field highlights one of the anomalies of writing instruction in the two-year colleges. This collection of essays attempts to frame the issues that make the two-year college a critical and contested site for understanding and critiquing the composition industry.

Our hope is that these essays will lead to both a serious reconsideration of composition in the two-year college and the creation of a new type of intellectual work in and about two-year colleges. Even the popular conceptions of the value of teaching and the democratic bent of these institutions need to be examined in the context of the kinds of literacy they promote and the social and political status of the students they presume to educate. Teaching in the two-year college has been invisible intellectual work, usually driven by theories and practices generated from university campuses a long way from the students and faculty at two-year institutions. Two-year college faculty often end up being gatekeepers for standards they did not create and do not control.

As the process model of composition wobbles on the brink of evolution or extinction, two-year college writing faculty face an uncertain future. As theorists begin to move away from the process model and toward theories that can variously be described as rhetorical, pragmatic, or semiotic, the uneasy sense that composition is an intensely local construction places the earlier, universalized notions in jeopardy. From this perspective, the differences between both the practitioners and the institutions that comprise the composition industry are an important site of critical analysis. Nowhere are the differences more pronounced and less discussed than in the two-year colleges, where composition often occupies a very different social pedagogical space than it does in four-year institutions.

Although there is no party line that ties these essays together, they all help define the specific material and social conditions that make composition in the two-year colleges unique and problematic. In a post-process approach to composition, those conditions define the contingencies, assumptions, and practices of literacy in these institutions. The differences are important because, as J. Elspeth Stuckey makes clear, language and literacy often mark social and economic differences:

> Said generally, language changes or emerges not via attention to language but according to the purposes of people in social relationships with one another. Where there is inequity in those relationships, there is inequity in language, and it is there for all the world to understand because it is on the outside. (91)

Thus, literacy and literacy practices are never neutral constructs. They are always marked by social and material conditions that call them into play. The process model of composition naturalized the literacy practices it endorsed, creating the convenient fiction that Donald Murray's writing conferences were essentially the same as the writing conferences of a marginalized, part-time instructor working for embarrassingly low wages at the local community college. In fact, very different literacy practices and a very different sense of academic capital distinguish these examples. The valorization of the process model by publishing companies further occluded the differences and helped put a humane face on an otherwise objectionable and problematic set of circumstances. The likelihood is that the same scarcity of resources that drives the unacceptably high rate of part-time faculty at the two-year colleges will push them toward an assessment program mass marketed by a major testing service, further alienating students and faculty from pedagogical and curricular decisions. Literacy practices at two-year colleges today often resemble the "hidden curriculum of work" that Jean Anyon found in high school English classes in the 1970s. Like the working-class students in Anyon's examples, two-year college students often face a workbook-driven approach, which assumes and punishes lapses in linguistic etiquette, while doing little to help them understand or contextualize the literacy practices of either the academy or wider social discourse. For many of these students, literacy is what John Mayer calls a "common-sense" construction, a view that promotes exclusion from higher-order literacy or thinking skills for the smallest transgressions. Cohen and Brawer have estimated that a third of community-college students are shuffled into remedial or developmental programs from which few of them ever emerge. The writing requirement is a critical factor in sorting out students, confirming Evan Watkins' observation that school is "a place, with very few exceptions, where you learn your place" (258).

Two-year colleges have always had critics who challenged the role these institutions played in preparing students to transfer to four-year institutions and to move into the job market. Beginning with Stephen Zwirling's, *Second Best,* and continuing through Kevin Dougherty's, *The Contradictory College,* these critics have focused on the way two-year colleges have provided, in the words of Brint and Karabel, a way of "managing ambition," of lowering the hopes and expectations of their students. The image of windowless basement classrooms with loud ceiling fans and gray tuna sandwiches in the cafeteria helped define what Ira Shor called the "budget colleges," a place where even the surroundings reminded the students that social class was not just an issue but *the* issue. The essays in this volume provide evidence that composition is a large part of that message, making literacy and writing a barrier to be overcome. Not surprisingly, students fall victim to the linguistic and cultural markers they bring in the door. It is still true that only about 12 percent of two-year college students ever graduate.

Clearly, the conditions facing composition faculty in the two-year colleges make it unlikely that they can change the system on their own. The treatment (if not exploitation) of part-time faculty, the reliance on the textbook publishers to frame the writing course and set goals, and the lack of two-year college faculty participation in the field all lead to a deskilling and devaluing of two-year college composition faculty. These conditions lead, unfortunately, to the conclusion that anybody can teach composition, an attitude shared by far too many community-college administrators. In this situation, it is critical to make the material conditions that mark the site of composition in the two-year colleges part of the dialogue.

Our goal in this book is to challenge the kinds of literacy practices that the material and political conditions within the two-year colleges promote. Although part of the CrossCurrents series, *The Politics of Writing in the Two-Year College* is also a response to Bullock and Trimbur's *The Politics of Writing Instruction: Postsecondary,* which Bullock and Trimbur note in their preface is rarely concerned with two-year college writing instruction. By providing critical insight into the way composition is situated and practiced in the two-year colleges, we hope to promote a broader discussion about what kind of literacy is being promoted.

In *The Long Revolution,* Raymond Williams outlined a historical relationship between literacy and democracy, arguing that advancements in the former invariably led to improvements in the latter. He warns that without vigilance, access, and education that correlation is not guaranteed to continue. With 50 percent of all first year college students and over 40 percent of all undergraduates taking composition courses in two-year colleges, these institutions seem a likely place to start asking ourselves what kind of literacy the composition requirement promotes. If we, as the voice of our profession, value a literacy that is democratic, inclusive, and critical, we will start by focusing on the two-year colleges.

Barry Alford

Works Cited

Anyon, J. 1980. "Social Class and the Hidden Curriculum of Work." *Journal of Education.* 162 (Winter).

Brint, S., & J. Karabel. 1989. *The Directed Dream.* New York: Oxford UP.

Bullock, R., & J. Trimber. 1991. *The Politics of Writing Instruction:Postsecondary.* Portsmouth, N.H.: Boynton/Cook.

Cohen, A. M., & F. Brawer. 1982. *The American Community College.* San Francisco: Jossey-Bass.

Cohen, H. & C. Ignash. 1992. "Trends in the Liberal Arts Curriculum." *Community College Review.* 50–56.

Dougherty, K. J. 1994. *The Contradictory College: The Conflicting Origins, Impacts, and Features of the Community College.* Albany: SUNY P.

Mayer, J. 1990. *Uncommon Sense: Theoretical Practice in Language Education.* Portsmouth, N.H.: Boynton/Cook.

Shor, I. 1977. *Critical Teaching and Everyday Life.* Chicago: U Chicago P.

Stuckey, J. E. 1991. *The Violence of Literacy.* Portsmouth. N.H.: Boynton/Cook.

Watkins, E. 1989. *Work Time.* Stanford: Stanford UP.

Williams, R. 1961. *The Long Revolution.* New York: Columbia UP.

Zwerling, L. S. 1976. *Second Best: The Crisis of the Junior College.* New York: McGraw-Hill.

1

Just a Little Higher Education

Teaching Working-Class Women on the Vocational Track

Eileen Ferretti

Before I came to college, I worked as a lunchroom mother at the Catholic elementary school my children attended in Bensonhurst, Brooklyn. Lunchroom mother was a position of only fragile authority. In reality, I was an illusion, a pseudomom, a make-believe institutional mother who had no real power. But my role required that I fill in for real authority (regular teachers) during the lunch hour, so I was often left to supervise the children without being supervised myself. Watching the kids required some spontaneous decision-making on my part, but, mostly, it required common sense, parental intuition, and peace-keeping skills. At the same time, this hour of standing in for the teachers created a potential breach in the power hierarchy between the credentialed school professionals who had real authority to make decisions and the uncredentialed people like me who did not. Some mothers helped in the classrooms and had the benefit of an authority figure (the teacher) close at hand to validate their decisions, much like dad backs up mom's decisions in the family at home. In the lunchroom, however, I was left to fight my own battles with the children without real authority, under the thumb of the dreaded Sister Superior who headed the school and who questioned my decisions at some awkward moments. My access to the shared assumptions and language practices of the professionals was limited. So, on those occasions when my spontaneous decisions were questioned, I related to the Sister Superior in two ways: submissive silence or rapid-fire rationalizations. Being silenced made me feel suppressed rage, while spontaneously justifying my behavior to the Sister Superior forced me to engage in a stressful (and frustrating) verbal performance.

When I look back on this chapter in my life, one particular day always comes to mind. We were in the midst of our monthly pizza sale, a very popular meal for the kids, so the lunchroom was overcrowded with children who usually went home to eat. I noticed that one fourth-grade boy was busy constructing a "homemade bomb"—an orange wrapped up in pieces of aluminum foil that were scattered about his lunch table. I caught him just as he was getting ready to throw the bomb at a group of first graders (to cover them with citrus splatter). So I disarmed him and placed him and his uneaten pizza at an empty table in the back of the lunchroom. As luck would have it, his mother was there selling pizza, and she threw a power bomb at me by reporting the incident to the Sister Superior who was right on the scene eyeballing me for an explanation. I stood there in the midst of spilled soda, empty cardboard boxes, and screaming children, trying to defend my unauthorized decision to isolate the little bomber. My rage exploded in words that pizza day, and I did such a good job at talking nonstop that Sister finally said, in exasperation, "Mrs. Ferretti, do you have a degree?" I said, "No, I have children."

Looking back on my brilliant career as a lunchroom mother, I know that the most important lesson I learned in the Catholic school cafeteria was that a college degree was important. It was a passport to respect, decision-making status, and some real authority. The second lesson I learned (several years later in the process of earning an advanced degree) was that the type of unequal schooling I had received in my working-class community of Bensonhurst[1] was actually constructed to prepare me for the position of lunchroom mother. About inequality, Jean Anyon[2] explains how schools make available differing and unequal educational experiences and curricula to students from different social classes. She found that in working-class schools, learning follows prescribed steps in a procedure that is usually mechanical, involving rote behavior and very little choice. Anyon's findings were later confirmed by Jeannie Oakes who notes, "Everywhere we turn, we see the likelihood of in-school barriers to upward mobility for capable poor and minority students."[3] In a later study of a first-grade class in an urban Appalachian school, Kathleen Bennett reported similar findings and came to the same conclusion, "They were continually told through classroom practices that they were the less capable, 'slower' students."[4] Further, the literacy narratives of successful working-class academics like Victor Villanueva, Keith Gilyard, and Mike Rose, report similar depressant experiences with working-class schooling.[5] As Mike Rose put it, "If you're a working-class kid on the vocational track you're defined by your school as slow, you're placed in a curriculum that isn't designed to liberate you, but to occupy you, or if you're lucky, to train you, though the training is for work the society does not esteem."[6] Like Rose, I did what I had to do to get by in school, but I did it with half a mind—the intellectual equivalent of playing with your food. As a lunchroom mother who yearned for the golden passport of a college degree, I had no idea that my working-class background and educational experiences had developed me to become a subordinate worker. I knew only that my prior education left me feeling bored, frustrated, and inadequate. Being a lunchroom mother fit right into my depressant education because school had already declared me unfit for college. Even though I had nagging intellectual desires, the lunchroom reenforced the notion that my aspirations for higher education were only pipe dreams. At the same time, as a subordinate worker in an educational setting, I was in daily contact with school professionals where I could see with my adult eyes the process of sorting and labeling children as "smart" or "slow." My growing awareness of this tracking process led to my own resistance to subordination and ended in my decision to leave the land of the dreaded Sister Superior, pizza sales, and juvenile bombers and go to Brooklyn College. At Brooklyn, a four-year liberal arts campus, I gained access to the elite track of higher education, one meant for the privileged few, not the masses. Released from the lunchroom, my new role as a student studying Western Civilization encouraged me to voice opinions, make decisions, negotiate points of difference, and imagine possibilities, rather than live with low expectations, "waiting to be told what to do and what things mean,"[7] as Ira Shor wrote in *Empowering Education.* I discovered that I might not be "unfit for college" after all.

Today, I'm an assistant Professor of English and co-director of Developmental Reading and Writing at Kingsborough Community College (CUNY) but being a lunchroom mother still feels too close for comfort. During my years in graduate school, I taught college writing to a group of paraprofessional women (or paras, as they are known at their job sites) employed by the New York City Board of Education to assist teachers in the classrooms as well as to provide supervision of children in the school cafeteria, on school buses, and in the playgrounds. In the case of children with special needs, the women act as custodial guardians, communication facilitators, and teacher-parent liaisons. Like me, these women come to higher education as the products of working-class schooling, and like me in the lunchroom, they occupy subordinate positions in a school setting where they have limited access to the assumptions and language practices of the professional class. But, unlike me, the paras are in college not to earn a liberal-arts degree, but to obtain Board Certification in their job title, which requires them to have a high-school diploma plus eight college credits within two years of employment.

When I first met them in my freshman writing class in 1992, the women informed me that most paras remain in college beyond eight credits solely to accumulate various electives in education and related fields for which they receive tuition waivers and regular salary increases.[8] After their long-term odyssey with career-based classes,[9] only some of them finally enter the liberal-arts track of the college and become my students in freshman composition or basic writing. Because their vocational curriculum is developed for full-time workers, most of whom are expected to remain at their present jobs, the difference between the expectations of their Board of Education program and the official degree requirements of the college is substantial. Thus, although these (upwardly mobile) liberal-arts paras represent the scholastic survivors in a group where most don't get that far, they are not on a fast track to academic learning, and their delayed entry into liberal-arts presents a range of conflicts for women already encumbered by full-time jobs and family responsibilities.

This essay reports on the politics of transition the paras encounter as they contemplate the leap from vocational career-based classes to the liberal-arts track of the college. Through the lens of the paras' classroom narratives and my teaching journal, I will offer a detailed account of their first two weeks in my freshman writing class in the fall of 1992. These written records of our initial classroom negotiations and dialogues also illuminate the politics of para culture I encountered in my attempts to reposition these women from workers who attend college for narrow technical knowledge (and pay raises) to student intellectuals who aspire to a liberal-arts degree. At the same time, in this classroom of women students who work for a living, I came face to face with the politics of academic culture—and its complicity in a tracking system that confines so many working-class and non-traditional students, like the paras, to the margins of the university.

Conflicting Expectations:
The Paras Confront Critical Pedagogy

Our first classroom encounter illuminated a shared history as working-class wives and mothers, subordinate workers in a school setting, and adult college students, and prompted me to question them about their everyday lives and their academic progress. Their answers provided material I thought would be useful to help them mediate between the limited vocational curriculum of their immediate past and the liberal-arts classes lying ahead. Thus, my pedagogy for the paras (drawn from the work of Paulo Freire and Ira Shor)[10] centers on a critical inquiry into their lives, issues, and concerns. Eager to use their observations and comments on their everyday lives as material for critical discussions and reflective inquiry,[11] I wanted to involve the women in all aspects of planning the curriculum. However, I soon discovered that the paras had their own plans for my freshman writing class. Assertive amid their subordination, these long-term veterans of the community-college system let me know right away that after an hour of "explaining para life" to me, they wanted an official (teacher-generated) syllabus, a detailed list of the written assignments, and an early dismissal—in that order. They preferred to maintain the structure of their career-based classes where required texts and written assignments were clearly outlined in black and white. Because they have thus far been trained and disciplined on the college campus to remain at the lower end of the job structure, to follow the orders of those above them, and to look to expert authorities for facts and information, they believe that education is a process of learning how to do things from those who know best, and they wanted me, the teacher-expert to give them quick instructions that they could use. Thus, my suggestion that we stay for the remaining class hour and codevelop the curriculum[12] was met with suspicion, even outright protest. (I would later learn that the teacher's formal syllabus represents a starting point from which the group typically initiates a downward negotiation of the workload.) At the first class, however, they told me that a detailed syllabus and semester-long assignment sheets are essential to their survival in college because they provide a certain measure of predictability and structure, which they believe allows them to do their schoolwork while raising families and working fulltime. Janice,[13] a thirty-six-year-old mother of three explained the group's perceived need for what she called "a specific map of the course requirements."

> Although we paras are in freshman composition, we are not typical college freshmen, we are different[14] . . . we are wives, mothers, and full-time workers who chose to enter liberal-arts courses after successful completion of a specialized curriculum. Our lives demand that we plan our schoolwork in advance so that college attendance fits into the larger picture.

This "larger picture" was described by most paras as commitments to other roles, which placed limits on their time and energy. "Given such hectic schedules," they said, "planning ahead for school assignments is a practical necessity." In addition, the women pointed out that the sequential structure of their program left them no option but to take three liberal-arts courses required for their Education Associate degrees (two in composition and one in literature, one in history, and one in philosophy) at the end of the vocational sequence. Thus, they did not expect the rules of college to change at this late date. Cassandra, a thirty-one-year-old African-American single mother of six explained the dilemma:

> The paras in this class want more out of college than a bigger paycheck. After spending so much time here, we want an associate degree. The only thing standing between us and that degree is three liberal-arts classes. We don't want or need any changes in our program, we just want you to give us a manageable workload outlined in a semester-long syllabus and an instruction sheet for each assignment.

Cassandra's comment indicates how the paras viewed my freshman writing class as doing time on the liberal-arts track (in exchange for a degree) in much the same way as they had done time on the vocational track (in exchange for pay raises). Acquisition of intellectual capital was not meaningful to them, as they preferred to accumulate more immediate, concrete rewards from the system (specific credentials leading to pay increases). Cassandra's comment also reveals the paras' habituation into the existing orthodoxies of the standard school curriculum where official textbooks and syllabi are dispensed by the teacher. Most of the women agreed with Cassandra, some saying, "It's your job to give us the work, and it's our job to do it." So, after each para had completed an introductory self-portrait,[15] I sent them home—without a syllabus or an assignment sheet. "What do you want us to bring to the next class?" they asked as they hurried out of the room, and I replied, "Just bring yourselves."

Later that evening, I pored over their written statements looking for recurrent impressions of para life (what Freire would call "generative themes").[16] To my surprise, "being silenced"[17] emerged as the most striking image (the "culture of silence" in the lives of the subordinate that Freire has written much about). Expressed variously and in different contexts, the subordination of the paras' own needs and voices to the expectations of others characterized their individual self-portraits. For example, some mentioned husbands who wanted a second income from their wives without the inconvenience that a wife's absence from home inevitably creates. As Joan, a thirty-four-year-old mother of three and a former New York City bus driver wrote, "Home life is easier when *he* doesn't see evidence (like dust on the coffee table) that I work." Others described their roles as workers and students as "a sore point at home," something best left "outside the family." Lin, a thirty-year-old Asian American mother of three, married to a Hispanic high school teacher, described her work and school identities as "aspects of myself best left at the door when I return to the family." I was also struck by the limited scope of these self-portraits, as the women described themselves solely in terms of the roles they play in relation to others. Janice, a thirty-six-year-old mother of three, captured the collective attitude quite well when she wrote, "I'm a wife to my husband, a mother to my three boys, a para to a first-grade class, and a student in the Ed. Associate Degree Program. . . . That's how most people would describe me. . . . There isn't much time left over for me to think about how I would describe myself, so I'm not sure how to write this kind of self-portrait." That night I wrote in my teaching journal:

> The women's writing reveals only who they are in relation to other people . . .
> not one para described her physical appearance or personality (how she looks,
> feels, thinks, or behaves)[18] and no one mentioned personal goals or profes-
> sional aspirations for the future. . . . Despite the outward appearance of col-
> lective strength and unity, the paras present themselves, individually, as *silent*
> *facilitators of other people's lives.*

Moving out of Imposed Silence

In the days that followed, I presented an invitation to compose autobiographical journals and reflective narratives on readings as a part of an overall critical curriculum that the women would codevelop with me. As soon as I made it clear that these classroom journals would count as a legitimate component of their assigned writing for the course, the paras agreed to participate in this enterprise — that is, to codevelop two forms of narrative productions and to dedicate an hour of class time each week to composing and sharing them. After some debate, the women chose "family," "work," and "student life" as the themes for their autobiographical narratives because these topics had already emerged in their classroom discussions of their day-to-day experiences. The other themes for their reflective narratives on readings (gender issues, class conflicts, and race relations) gradually took shape from the issues raised in their autobiographical texts. Reading materials for these narrative responses were chosen from three sources: a collection of articles the women brought to class from popular magazines such as *Redbook* and *Ladies Home Journal;* editorials on current events from newspapers; and essays distributed in their sociology, psychology, and education classes. To supplement these student selections, I introduced articles from the anthology *One World, Many Cultures*.[19] Finally, the paras chose Toni Morrison's *The Bluest Eye*[20] from the departmentally approved list of full-length works for freshman writing.

This part of the negotiation process went smoothly; the paras worked in small groups on selected themes, and I compiled and organized their articles to compose a reading list and a course outline. Although the final document was extensive, I assumed that we would use it as a *guide*, adding or subtracting material as the interests and concerns of the students emerged throughout the semester. However, as I distributed the long-awaited syllabus, the paras moved from stunned silence to loud protest in less than a minute. A few retrieved calculators from their bags and tallied the number of pages in the reading selections. Others suggested that I used the idea of small groups to divide and conquer the class; that is, I encouraged each group to work independently, so no one saw the total picture until it was too late. The paras let me know right away that they were angry, not because I had imposed a difficult syllabus on them, but because I had *used them* to collaborate on a long syllabus they could not and would not live with. I would later learn that the mutual process had pre-preempted their routine downward negotiation of the workload between instructor and students, forcing the paras to negotiate with each other, or, as they put it, "to fight for the articles they wanted to read and the themes they wanted to explore." To negotiate through their resistance to their own big syllabus, I suggested that the women form special-interest groups, one for each topic. The members of each group would review the readings on a particular topic and then report back to the class on their findings. In this way, every article would be read and evaluated, but only some selections would be assigned to the class. Happy with this decreased workload, the women quickly organized three committees on gender, class, and race relations to review the reading material.

It's Not a "Problem," It's My "Reality": Inscribing the Facts of Para Life

Initially, the paras used their autobiographical narratives on home, work, and student life to record their life experiences. They did not view the role conflicts that surfaced in these texts as problems, but, rather, as facts of life to be documented in their journals and confirmed through dialogue with other paras in the room. Pedagogically, I structured the recurrent themes as material I wanted to pose as problems[21] for changing their aspirations, intellectual habits, and literacy style. To be concrete about how I use problem-posing, I can report on the women's initial interpretations of their autobiographical texts and my attempts to re-present their accounts from multiple perspectives. From the start, I wanted the paras to be active and thoughtful, to examine their narrative accounts from their own points of view. At the same time, I wanted them to take a critical attitude toward their own experiences, that is, to raise questions about their own subjectivity in relation to their stories. Thus, pedagogically, my aim was to foster an awareness of their stories as localized accounts that relate to larger social issues. To encourage multiple perspectives, I asked each member of the class to compose an autobiographical narrative in which she defined two of her roles in relation to each other. Some paras wrote humorous caricatures of their *transformation* (as they put it) from "Mary Poppins" at their school job sites to "Cinderella's stepmother" at home. As Janice wrote, "There's only so much patience to go around —and my own kids are always last in line." Others offered more serious and concrete evidence of their role conflicts, telling stories of latchkey children, domestic violence, divorce, and bitter custody battles. A memorable example of the difference between the humorous and the more serious approach to role conflict emerged in the narratives of Stephanie and Cassandra. Stephanie, a thirty-eight-year-old Italian American mother of four wrote an account of conflict between her domestic and working lives, which centered on a family protest over how her going to work "left the dog home alone all day." By contrast, Cassandra's narrative about coming to college as a single mother related an episode of sibling rivalry that ended with "fourteen-year-old Beverly locking five-year-old Shaneka in the closet one night while Mommy was at school."[22]

Initially, I was struck by the contrast presented in these two accounts. Even more surprising, however, was the women's matter-of-fact presentation and the paras' humorous response to them. Clearly, Stephanie saw her social construction in the family (companion to the dog) as an insult to her domestic role and an unpleasant alternative to working outside the home, but her narrative made no reference to the more significant conflicts inherent in her daily life as a working mother with four school-aged children. While Cassandra openly admitted that her older daughter is angry about taking care of younger siblings, she viewed her situation not as a function of her status as an African American single mother who cannot afford adequate child care but as an "inevitable" conflict between a parent and a teenager. Thus, instead of situating their roles in relation to each other, the paras' first narratives offered episodes of family life in which the underlying social, cultural, gender, and class conflicts were left unexplored. In addition, the obvious disparities (of economics, race, and marital status) encoded in these different accounts of family life (stories that explicitly defined the diverse and unequal realities among the paras) were absent from the women's discussion of their texts.

My pedagogical goal at this point was twofold. First, it was necessary to acknowledge these narratives as meaningful representations of the literacies and life experiences the women brought with them to class. Second, it was important to re-present[23] their stories to them, calling attention to the operative forces of class, gender, race, and ethnicity that impact their lives. To accomplish the first objective, I made sure that each narrative was read and discussed in class —even though some of the paras felt that their "issue" had been raised (and resolved) through commentary on previous narratives.[24] As Pat Belanoff suggests, "Pulling students away from the particulars of their lives, their stories of themselves, may create crippling disjunctions in their lives outside of school. And acceding to the possibility that we cannot change any of this until the world outside changes may cripple us."[25] Although I took notes on these first narratives, I did not immediately attempt to synthesize student responses while the class was in session. Instead, I asked the women to write a follow-up journal entry that explored one aspect of culture (race, ethnicity, social class, family, religion, media, education, and so on) that they believed influenced the story they told. In this way, the paras were able to actively participate in my second objective— re-presenting their own stories.

The follow-up journal entries helped me synthesize the material from the paras' first narratives. For example, Janice's lighthearted account of being "Mary Poppins" to other people's children at school, only to turn into "Cinderella's stepmother" at home illustrated a conflict between her roles as a worker and a mother. In her follow-up journal, she recast the conflict in ways that suggested how educational and social forces influenced her behavior. Although clearly disorganized and rambling, her text alluded to the power of unconscious mechanisms that operate on us in different social contexts—a theme that the class was eager to examine. Janice opened her narrative by defining her dual role (working mother) as one complicated and frustrated by the "sameness of duties." At the same time, she acknowledged that the "same duties" elicited two different kinds of behavior from her. "The 'Mary Poppins' of P.S. 212," she wrote, "would suffer the unfortunate consequence of being fired if she lost her cool at school, while the 'Cinderella's stepmother' of Benson Avenue would lose her mind if she didn't lose her cool once in a while at home." Janice chose *education* as the cultural force that influenced her roles as a mother and a worker. Specifically, she said that she enacted what she called "textbook techniques" in the classroom, but relied, at home, on the parenting practices she remembered from her own upbringing. To my surprise, many of the women admitted that, like Janice, they divided child care into two patterns of behavior: what they called *learned response* at school versus *natural response* at home. This commentary introduced a conflict between the communication techniques that the paras learned in college and the child-rearing patterns they actually believed in and practiced at home. Some said that they tried to apply the knowledge they acquired in their education classes to their relationships with their own children, but found the difficulties almost insurmountable. Valerie, a forty-six-year-old mother of two teenage sons summarized a masculine obstacle many paras faced at home when she said:

> Reasoned verbal communication does work best in the long-run if it has been an ongoing process in the child's life and everyone agrees that it's the right thing to do. Unfortunately, my husband has a violent temper and a short fuse.

> In my house, if I don't yell at the boys sufficiently, my husband will hit them.
> I'm afraid that at ages 13 and 15, they might someday hit him back, so I yell—
> sufficiently—to defuse the situation.

Although I wanted to continue working on these self-generated texts, some of the paras, ever mindful of the syllabus, reminded me that our next narrative session would focus on their first reflective narratives on selected readings.

Between Storytelling and Academic Writing: Negotiating the Boundaries

Some of the paras were eager to begin the narrative reflections on readings, but others felt that it was "too early" to incorporate outside sources into their journal writing. Joan, the former bus driver expressed most clearly the paras' need to separate their personal narratives from academic writing. She noted that narratives and essays require different composing styles, describing these distinctions in a journal entry titled "Interpreting and Translating Stories":

> Writing about my life and hearing other paras' stories . . . helped me to connect
> different kinds of experience and to interpret how one part of my story is linked
> to another . . . In formal papers, though, I find myself struggling to "translate"
> the authors' meaning. I don't feel that I can interpret their experiences (which
> are different from mine). . . . The best writing I've ever done is in my personal
> journal, and I don't want it to become a book of essays that I don't know how
> to write.

Indeed, Joan's narrative provided an accurate description of the paras' formal essays, which, so far, had been unimaginative brief documents lacking the depth and clarity I had come to expect from their journals. However, the fact that Joan characterized her autobiographical narratives as complex representations of her life confirmed their importance from a pedagogical, as well as a personal perspective. As J. Blake Scott notes, "Literacy narratives, by their very nature, provide a forum in which students can develop metacommunicative critiques of themselves and others." [26] The paras' autobiographical accounts disrupted a set of separate experiences bringing their multiple roles into contact with each other and bringing the women in touch with the complexities of their lives. Thus, I could see the benefit of preserving the nonacademic discourse in their narrative productions. At the same time, I hoped that the narrative reflections on readings would provide a transition from illuminating para culture to an entry into the larger world of literature, what Sondra Perl calls "new tales and tellings called out by the stories of others." [27]

To negotiate this transition, I suggested that we codevelop some guidelines for reflective narratives that would preserve the boundaries between narrative productions and academic writing. The women voiced their concerns about negotiating the borders between articulating personal experience and commenting on outside sources. I recognized that personal experience was relevant to their reflective journals and I encouraged them to incorporate it into this new journal format. I also reminded them that these narratives on outside readings were not intended to replace their autobiographical journals but merely to supplement and enhance them. As the tone of this discussion suggests, despite the women's limited experience with college writing, they already approached composing in much the same way as Pamela Annas described our teacherly response to it: "We may value women's creative writing while at the same time feel that it is very different from expository writing, . . . which we have been trained to think should be based on what the authorities say rather than on personal experience."[28]

After we established consensus on the format for the narrative reflections, the paras chose Toni Morrison's *The Bluest Eye* as the first reading selection because they felt that the novel presented all of the themes (gender, race, and class) that their reflections would address and provided the best opportunity to discuss them from multiple perspectives. The women reminded me that the book was 216 pages long and suggested that the first journals be confined to the preface to allow the students a week to read and reflect on the rest of the novel; I agreed. To maintain the familiarity of our narrative sessions, I kept my approach consistent with the one I used for the autobiographical journals. Each para was invited to read from her written response; I took notes and asked the women to comment. Angelica, a forty-two-year-old Hispanic mother of four, volunteered to go first:

> In the opening passage of *The Bluest Eye,* Toni Morrison writes about an average American family playing ball in the backyard. . . . She uses short, simple sentences to introduce the young narrator . . . Claudia MacTeer. . . . The gradual disappearance of punctuation and word-spacing represents the author's attempt to introduce the theme of "family dysfunction" in the novel.

Because one of my pedagogical goals for the reflective narratives is to foster what Linda Christensen calls, "An ability to switch in and out of the language of the powerful,"[29] I was encouraged by Angelica's movement in this brief text from summary to analysis and interpretation. At the same time, I noticed that she limited her commentary to the formal (third-person) voice. There was no "I" in her text and no connection between her own experience and the family scene she interpreted.

By contrast, the paras' response to her journal centered on Angelica's use of the term "dysfunctional" and the assumptions it made about the families in the novel.[30] Cassandra was particularly disturbed by what she called Angelica's "labeling" of the African American families in the novel as "dysfunctional." She then proceeded to read her own narrative, titled "Black and White," in which she argued that the "normal" family in the opening passage represents the "white" family, an "ideal" to which all of the black families are negatively compared. "As an African American woman," she wrote, "I was upset to see that a well-known

black author created no positive images of black people in this novel." This
statement was immediately challenged by other women who viewed the African
American MacTeer family as stable and supportive, if not "ideal." Many of the
white paras (who were visibly uncomfortable with the topic of race relations)
raised objections to Cassandra's assumption that the "storybook" family in the
preface is white (because race is never mentioned in the passage). Janice's comments summed up this opinion:

> The difference between the ideal family in the preface and the families in the
> novel is money. . . . People who live in "very pretty green and white houses"
> have money, people who live in "broken down houses with cracks in the win-
> dows" don't have money. It's money that separates the storybook family from
> the families in the novel, not race.

Janice's attempt to "deracinate" the text by substituting "class" only added
to Cassandra's fury. She would not be silenced and countered Janice's remark
with the quip, "How many of you black women would name your kids Dick and
Jane? . . . Get real, Janice, this ideal family is white." Janice responded by asking, "How many of us white women would name our kids Dick and Jane? . . ."
The passage represents the fictional all-American family of the past—like
Leave it to Beaver and *Father Knows Best.* "Yeah," Cassandra countered, "rich
white families." Janice conceded this point, and Cassandra had the last word.

   This heated discussion had illuminated the intersections of race and class
(an issue that I wanted to pose as a problem for critical inquiry). However, before moving forward to a discussion of how race and class are portrayed in the
preface (on the basis of only two narratives), I decided to bring the paras back
to reading from their own texts. To do this, I asked them to take notes on each
narrative and to hold their comments until everyone had a chance to share some
lines from her journal. As the women read their responses, it became obvious
that the class was indeed divided along racial lines, but that the split involved
more than a response to the material in the preface. Gloria, a thirty-eight-year-
old African American mother of five illuminated the gap between one group of
paras and the other:

> You have to read the whole book to understand the preface. . . . some of us
> have done that in basic writing. Our instructor spent a lot of time connecting
> the preface to the novel, and some of the narratives in this class reflect this in-
> structor's ideas. For the sake of those who did not read the novel yet, I think
> we should compose our narratives on the preface.

I thanked Gloria for sharing this information with me and offered her proposal to the class. Most of the women (who were at various points in the book)
said that the preface was "too short" and acquired most of its meaning from the
text that followed it. I used this opportunity to pose a question for narrative
reflection on the preface (which I thought contained a great deal of material
to be mined). I asked the women to form four groups and suggested that each

group devise a definition of the "average American family" as it is depicted in the preface. Although members of individual groups reached consensus rather quickly, significant variance appeared between groups. The first group asserted that the passage depicted a "higher socioeconomic class," not the "average American family" as they knew it: "Toni Morrison is describing a well-to-do family with a backyard and lots of leisure time for parents and children to play together." The second group saw the depiction of the two-parent family with one boy, one girl, a dog, and a cat as a stereotypical image of the "nuclear family:" "The author is describing the ideal family with two parents, two kids, and two pets, not the average American family." The third group noted the "laughing mother" and the "smiling father" as the most significant aspect of the passage because the concept of "domestic bliss" is part of the great American myth of family life. They argued, "The passage describes the 'happy' family, not the 'average' family." The fourth group asserted that Morrison describes the "average American family" as we know it from the media. They concluded, "The family in the passage is an accurate reflection of the 'model' that all American families aspire to become, even though most are not."

I was impressed by the multiple levels of theorizing in the group's conceptualizations of the "American family" in this short passage. "If all of these interpretations are valid," I asked, "then where is the thematic center (the main idea) in the preface—and who is this family?" Using their collective definitions as a guide, the paras listed the most significant qualities of the family as economically secure, two-parent, happy, and adored by American culture. After some deliberation, Stephanie suggested, "The thematic center is the idea that Morrison makes up a family that seems familiar to all of us, but isn't representative of most of us. That is, it's familiar because . . . it's the way life is supposed to be, but more often than not, it's not that way." Other women noted that it's familiar to those of us who grew up in the 1950s and 1960s when television made us believe that "everyone lived that way."

Through these interpretations of the model family, I saw that the paras were constructing a "theory" of their world(s)—the ideal world that they are supposed to be living in versus the one they inhabit. In this exercise, they were performing critical literacy, that is, "reading the world and the word," as Freire put it. Still, there remained one more issue to confront, the intersection of race and class that had launched our critical inquiry. To re-present this question, I asked the women to examine the four characteristics they assigned to the family in the preface and to write a reflective narrative that offered some suggestions on how race and class are implicated in these social markers. The first (financially secure) was easy—everyone agreed it's a class issue. The second (two-parent) presented multiple layers of interpretation. Some of the women wrote narratives that pointed to the rise in single-parent households across racial groups and the increase in the number of black middle-class families. As Joan put it, "Having two parents is no longer a 'given' if you are white—and no longer 'unusual' if you are black." Others suggested that race was still a primary distinction in single-parent households. For example, pointing to the "lack of male support for African American women," Cassandra wrote of the "sexual irresponsibility" that she feels permeates African American (male) culture and contributes to the confinement of most African American families to poorer groups. Citing material from her sociology textbook, she wrote, "Statistically, African American families are more likely to be poor . . . and more likely to be headed by females. . . . Therefore, race is implicated in Morrison's depiction of the two-parent family." The third quality (happiness) was seen by some women as irrelevant to both race and class. As Lin wrote, "I used to be a housekeeper in Hong Kong. This lady I worked for and all of her friends were miserable. I would not want to live her life." Others, like Gloria, disagreed: "Financial security does not guarantee happiness, but the scene depicted in this preface would not be possible without money. . . . Poor people (white or black) have no time to play with their kids and no yard to play in. . . . Therefore, class (but not race) is implicated in this depiction of 'domestic bliss'." Finally, (the model family created by the media) also received a mixed response. Angelica's narrative suggested that the "ideal" family depicted on television and in the movies is usually both wealthy and white. Stephanie disagreed, pointing to "The Huxtables" as the "ideal image" for black families, and concluded that "class supersedes race in Hollywood." What was most impressive about this exchange was the power of the text in mediating the paras' discussion of race and class. The women demonstrated a keen capacity to find and interpret textual evidence, which helped to defuse the racial polarity that had threatened to disrupt critical dialogue.

Conclusion

As my own journal notes reflect, I was overwhelmed by the amount of material written and discussed in the first two weeks. Fortunately, the paras became my partners in this critical enterprise, as individual voices continued to emerge from the collective chorus that greeted me on the first day of class. Stories were told, disagreements aired, and negotiation became the operative mode of classroom dialogue. However, at this point, I was also mindful of the delicate balance I had to maintain between storytelling and critical analysis, boundaries between personal narratives and academic discourse that I hoped the paras would transcend. I also hoped that "reading the word and the world" would illuminate one more set of critical questions that needed to be asked: Why is their world arranged like this? Who set it up? Who benefits from the inequality they encounter in family, work, and student life? Thus, I wanted critical reflection on previously unreflected experiences to encourage them to take what Jerome Bruner calls a "stance" toward their material.[31] A critical stance toward their generative themes may also bring them to what Freire calls "a perception of their previous perceptions,"[32] or rewriting the reality which has so far kept them subordinate in all the spaces of their lives.

Notes

1. Although I graduated from a Catholic elementary school at the top of my eighth-grade class, I was offered no option by the Diocese of Brooklyn but to attend an all-girls Catholic high school where I received mostly secretarial training from poorly educated nuns and female lay teachers. By contrast, a few top-ranked boys went on to elite academic programs designed exclusively for males. Thus, inequality was "gendered" as well as "classed"— upward mobility was difficult for boys and impossible for girls in my working-class community of Bensonhurst in the 1960s.

2. See J. Anyon (1992) "Social Class and the Hidden Curriculum of Work," in *Rereading America: Cultural Contexts for Critical Teaching and Writing,* ed. G. Colombo, R. Cullen, and B. Lisle (Boston: St. Martin's): 524 – 40, originally published in the *Journal of Education,* for a discussion of the characteristics of working-class school curricula.

3. See J. Oakes (1985) *Keeping Track: How Schools Structure Inequality* (New Haven: Yale UP): 134.

4. See K. Bennett (1991) "Doing School in an Urban Appalachian First Grade," in *Empowerment Through Multicultural Education,* ed. C. Sleeter (Albany: SUNY P): 46.

5. See V. Villanueva (1993) *Bootstraps* (Urbana, Ill: NCTE), K. Gilyard (1991) *Voices of the Self* (Detroit: Wayne State UP), and M. Rose (1990) *Lives on the Boundary* (New York: Penguin).

6. See M. Rose (1990) *Lives on the Boundary* (New York: Penguin): 28.

7. See I. Shor (1992) *Empowering Education* (Chicago: U of Chicago P): 18.

8. The New York City Board of Education remits tuition payments for up to six credits per semester for paras who major in education, and it awards yearly salary increases for every fifteen credits earned by paras up to a maximum of sixty.

9. I taught freshman and basic writing in the para program at Kingsborough over ten consecutive semesters (1992–97). The women in my classes averaged eight years of part-time attendance, accumulating between sixty and eighty vocational credits before they entered the liberal-arts track..

10. In *Empowering Education* (Chicago: U of Chicago P), Ira Shor (1992) defines critical pedagogy as a "democratic curriculum examining all subjects and learning processes with systematic depth, to connect student individuality to larger historical and social issues, to encourage students to examine how their experience relates to academic knowledge, to power, and to inequality in society, and to approach received wisdom and the status quo with questions" (16–17). See also P. McLaren (1989) *Life in Schools: An Introduction to Critical Pedagogy in the Foundations of Education* (New York: Longman); S. D. Brookfield (1987) *Developing Critical Thinkers: Challenging Adults to Explore Alternative Ways of Thinking and Acting* (San Francisco: Jossey-Bass); J. Banks (1981) *Multiethnic Education: Theory and Practice* (Boston: Allyn and Bacon); and J. Dewey (1966) *Democracy and Education* (New York: Free Press), originally published in 1916; P. Friere (1970) *Pedagogy of the Oppressed* (New York: Seabury).

11. With regard to method, I proceed by drawing material for critical inquiry from the students' verbal and written comments on their home, work, and school experiences. That is, what the students say and write about their own lives become the texts to be read

in class, and how members of the class respond to each other's stories provides the first means through which to interpret these texts.

12. I codevelop the curriculum with my students because it involves them in a decision-making process. No longer merely spectators or subordinates, they are invited to become participants in an educational setting. As Ira Shor (1992) points out in *Empowering Education,* "Education for empowerment is not something done by teachers to students for their own good, but something students codevelop for themselves led by a critical and democratic teacher" (20).

13. All of the paras gave me permission to use their classroom commentary and written journals in this essay. The names attached to particular excerpts are pseudonyms that each woman selected for herself. With the exception of standardizing spelling and punctuation and editing out repetitions (indicated by ellipses) I did not alter their verbal or written comments.

14. This difference became increasingly apparent to me during the semester. Although they had been given little access to habits of critical inquiry or to the language practices of the academy, the paras had acquired a great deal of information from their vocational courses. Their familiarity with sociological, psychological, and educational terms (and their curiosity about how to apply this knowledge in their everyday lives) provided a starting point from which to synthesize their observations and commentary into a focused discussion on the questions and issues they raised in class.

15. These self-portraits grew into the autobiographical accounts of home, work, and campus life that I discuss later in the essay.

16. "Generative themes" grow out of student culture and express problematic conditions in daily life that are useful for generating critical discussion. Freire (1978) discusses generative themes in *Pedagogy of the Oppressed* (New York: Continuum), and *Education for Critical Consciousness* (New York: Seabury). Ira Shor (1992) also discusses the generative theme method in *Empowering Education.* For a report on the use of generative themes in a writing curriculum designed for adult women in the Bahamas, see K. Fiore and N. Elsasser (1982) "Strangers No More: A Liberatory Literacy Curriculum," *College English* 44:115–28.

17. Although the paras were anything but silent during this first class session, I would later discover the same rhetorical conflicts among them that I experienced as a lunchroom mother. At times, these substantial women were silenced by just a few words from me the "teacher authority." Yet, there were moments when their voices erupted in a nonstop stream of words, as if they felt the need to articulate everything they had ever heard, thought, or felt before their brief time to speak in class ran out. Like myself in the lunchroom, they lacked confidence in their rhetorical authority while also lacking command of academic discourse. But, unlike me, the paras had remained in subordinate positions at work, so their lives required a continual negotiation between being a worker and being a college student—behavior and language practices that more often than not are at odds with each other.

18. In *Women's Ways of Knowing,* Mary Belenky et al. (1986) observed similar responses among a particular group of women they categorized as "silent." They reported, "Describing the self was a difficult task for all of the women we interviewed, but it was almost impossible for the silent ones. . . . They do not even provide a portrait of the physical self" (31–32).

19. S. Hirschberg ed. (1992) *One World, Many Cultures* (Needham Heights, MA: Allyn & Bacon).

20. T. Morrison (1992) *The Bluest Eye* (New York: Penguin), originally published in 1970.

21. In *Empowering Education,* Ira Shor (1992) defines "problem-posing" as a pedagogical approach that "offers all subject matter as historical products to be questioned rather than as universal wisdom to be accepted" (32). Shor points out, "The responsibility of the problem-posing teacher is to diversify subject matter and to use students' thought and speech as the base for developing critical understanding of personal experience, unequal conditions in society, and existing knowledge . . . posing knowledge in any form as a problem for mutual inquiry" (33).

22. These divergent accounts of working-class female experience raise the profile of race and marital status among the paras, while also calling attention to the various "caste positions" among these women, by which I mean the social and economic inequalities among working-class families. Specifically, Stephanie, a white woman married to a high-income electrician faced a "demeaning" show of family opposition to her working outside the home. Cassandra, a single, low-wage, African American mother faced the genuine and potentially dangerous rage of her older child who was left at home to babysit for younger siblings while their mother attended college for pay raises.

23. With regard to method, re-presenting the paras' stories involves synthesizing their statements and dialogue into questions and comments that focus on a problem for critical reflection. To do this, I take notes on their narratives and the class commentary on them. I read my notes back to them and ask them what questions and issues seem to be recurring and which ones they think we should focus on. I list their suggestions on the blackboard so that they can see the conversation they are hearing. After a number of key issues are presented by the students, I offer my own perceptions and suggestions about how we might proceed to the next level of inquiry.

24. Although some paras shared their views on everything, others had thus far remained silent. I wanted to ensure that each para established a voice in the classroom. Later in the term, the women volunteered to read their narratives (or parts thereof) to the class, and most offered material from them to me for comments. At the end of the term, each para submitted copies of her semester-long narrative productions, which comprised one-third of the grade in the course (assigned essays and the departmental final exam making up the remaining two-thirds).

25. See P. Belanoff (1993) "Language: Closings and Openings," in *Working-Class Women in the Academy,* ed. M. M. Tokarczyk and E. A. Fay (Amherst: U of Massachusetts P): 251–75.

26. See J. B. Scott (May 1997) "The Literacy Narrative as Production Pedagogy in the Composition Class," *Teaching English in the Two-Year College:* 108–117.

27. See S. Perl (1994) "Composing Texts, Composing Lives," *Harvard Educational Review* 64(4): 427–49.

28. See P. Annas (1985) "Style as Politics: A Feminist Approach to the Teaching of Writing," *College English* 47: 360–72.

29. See L. Christensen (Feb. 1990) "Teaching Standard English: Whose Standard?" *English Journal* 79 (Feb.): 36–40.

30. I would later learn that Angelica and some other paras who had previously taken developmental writing had already read and written essays on the book, and that they had been instrumental in the selection of this novel as our full-length reading (another way the paras downwardly negotiated the course workload).

31. See J. Bruner (1986) *Actual Minds, Possible Worlds* (Cambridge, Mass.: Harvard UP).

32. See P. Freire (1970) *Pedagogy of the Oppressed* (New York: Seabury): 108.

2

"Where We Are Is Who We Are"

Location, Professional Identity, and the Two-Year College

Karen Powers-Stubbs and Jeff Sommers

Jeff Sommers and Karen Powers-Stubbs have worked together since 1986 when Karen enrolled in one of Jeff's classes at the Middletown branch of Miami University of Ohio as a nontraditional undergraduate student. Jeff is now a tenured professor who teaches undergraduate students on the Middletown campus and graduate students on the main campus in Oxford. After finishing her undergraduate degree, Karen also taught on both campuses while she completed an M.A. and a Ph.D. in composition and rhetoric; she is currently an assistant professor at the Mansfield branch of The Ohio State University. Their conversations about composition, literature, and teaching, which began in a British literature survey course more than a decade ago, have evolved to reflect their changing theoretical, social, and geographic positions. The following interwoven narratives are typical of their conversations in that they explore dialogically "where they are" at this particular social and historical moment.

Toni Cade Bambara's "The Lesson," a story frequently anthologized and often taught at our campuses, depicts a field trip to an upscale toy store in New York taken by several young African American teenagers under the supervision of one of their neighbors, Miss Moore. Miss Moore's hope is that the children will learn something about how our culture has positioned them based on their living in Harlem. The story's narrator comments, "Where we are is who we are, Miss Moore always pointin' out. But it don't necessarily have to be that way" (53). Miss Moore hopes to encourage the children to think critically about their location in life so they might begin to change things for themselves.

When we began to think about writing this essay, we thought of Miss Moore and her charges. Miss Moore is the architect of the story's lesson, making her a teacher; however, she is not a licensed or certified teacher. Her "students" are rowdy and unruly and often resistant to her "lesson plans." The lesson takes place

19

in Harlem, a socioeconomically marginalized part of New York City. In all these ways, the story speaks analogously of the situation of two-year college faculty: viewed as somehow different and less as instructors, teaching in a less-desirable location, and working with less-prepared students. Miss Moore's lesson about location also makes a point relevant to the professional lives of two-year college faculty, who are viewed by both four-year faculty and the public as well as by themselves as "who they are" by virtue of "where they are." But, as Miss Moore's lesson suggests, things don't have to be that way.

As we have worked on this chapter, we have learned that we may not in fact be where we thought we were. To be more precise, this chapter is not going to turn out as we anticipated. Here is what we promised our editors:

"Where We Are Is Who We Are, But It Doesn't Have to Be That Way": Two- and Four-Year Faculty Discourse Communities

The title of the chapter comes from Toni Cade Bambara's short story, "The Lesson," frequently taught at our two-year campus. In Bambara's story, Miss Moore volunteers to educate the young teens of her Harlem neighborhood during their summer vacation from school. She takes them on a trip to FAO Schwarz, the upscale toy store in midtown Manhattan. The comment reflects Miss Moore's lesson for the children.

The short story serves as an analogy to the relationship we see between two- and four-year campus faculty. Like Miss Moore, two-year faculty do not always seem like "real" teachers, their students may not resemble traditional students, their lesson plans may follow a different model as well. In some ways, two-year faculty are members of a different discourse community than their colleagues at four-year campuses.

In this chapter, we will argue that the relationship between Miami's two-year branch campus at Middletown and its main four-year campus in Oxford, campuses at which we have both taught, can be seen as a microcosm of the relationship between two- and four-year campuses. The chapter will focus on the characteristics that differentiate the two discourse communities including the following:

- the effects of the campuses on promotion and tenure expectations in the areas of teaching, scholarship, and service
- the primary professional journals that serve each discourse community
- the colonizing effects of four-year campus faculty teaching extra courses at the two-year campus
- the student population of the two-year campus and how it defines faculty roles
- the shifts in identity required of teachers who teach at both campuses

What has changed for us is the bold-faced material because it no longer seems accurate to say that our position as faculty on a two-year branch campus of a four-year institution is analogous to the position of a community-college faculty member compared to faculty at the four-year campus nearby. A part-time community-college teacher, Katy Kysar, has commented on her position,

> I'm tired of a system that dictates a hierarchy: tenured professors who teach critical theory are at the top; nontenured M.A.'s who teach composition are in the basement; the college literature professors tenured at small, four-year colleges are stuck somewhere in the elevator around the fifth floor. (Nist & Raines, 298)

Vaughan (1994) also uses a geographical metaphor to locate community-college faculty in "that middle ground between four-year research institutions and high schools" (213). As we have worked on this essay, we have come to see ourselves located somewhere in the middle ground *between* the middle ground occupied by faculty at community colleges and the ground occupied by faculty at four-year institutions. In other words, we may be on the ground floor of Kysar's academic building.

Jane Peterson argues that two-year composition teachers are not homogeneous and that "we need to write our stories, tailoring them to specific audiences for specific purposes" (Nist & Raines 1993, 310). So we propose not to present our positions as a microcosm—that is, not to make generalizations—rather, we will particularize our own experiences and tell the stories of the positions each of us holds—one a tenured professor, the other an assistant professor just out of graduate school. In this chapter, we make no pretense of offering any definitive analyses of professional life on two-year or branch or four-year campuses. What we can offer is the stories of two professional lives in the making, stories that are not yet complete. Our chapter is not going to be an attempt at a master narrative. Indeed, properly speaking, we present no traditional conclusion at all, just a trailing off. Our intended audience is our colleagues at community colleges, branch campuses, and four-year institutions, and our purpose is to encourage a closer examination by all with an interest in Miss Moore's lesson: to learn what the extent that where we teach determines who we are.

Following is a brief description of the Middletown branch campus of Miami University. Miami is a state university in Oxford, Ohio, just inside the southwestern corner of Ohio, not far from the Indiana border. Founded in 1809, Miami offers its 16,000 undergraduates the opportunity to take degrees in arts and science, business, education, applied science, and interdisciplinary studies. Nine departments offer Ph.D.'s, including the English Department. In the 1960s, the governor of Ohio proclaimed as his goal that no state resident would live more than fifty miles from an institution of higher learning. Rather than create a statewide community-college system, Ohio created a system of branch campuses. Miami has two such branches, Middletown being the older of the two, founded in 1966. Approximately 2,200 students enroll at the Middletown campus, many for the same reasons students attend community colleges: our tuition is more affordable and our classes are smaller than four-year institutions, we offer associate degrees, and we prepare students to transfer to four-year institutions.

Approximately one hundred miles northeast of Oxford and Miami University is The Ohio State University (OSU), located in Columbus, the state capital.

Founded in 1870, Ohio State is one of the largest universities in the United States, offering more than 170 majors to more than 45,500 undergraduate students and more than 9,500 graduate and professional students. Students choose from fourteen colleges: Arts and Sciences; Business; Dentistry; Education; Engineering; Food, Agriculture, and Environmental Sciences; Human Ecology; Law; Medicine and Public Health; Nursing; Optometry; Pharmacy; Social Work; and Veterinary Medicine. The English Department, which Karen joined in 1999, offers a Ph.D., one of ninety-three degrees offered at Ohio State. In addition to the main campus in Columbus, Ohio State has five regional campuses, servicing central, northeast, and northwest sections of the state. Approximately 1,500 undergraduate students attend the Mansfield campus, enrolling at the campus midway between Columbus and Cleveland for many of the same reasons that students enroll at Miami–Middletown. Yet Mansfield differs in some significant ways from Middletown, as well as from other regional campuses in the Ohio State system. Students at Mansfield can complete all of the requirements for bachelor's degrees in elementary education, psychology, and English at that campus. Students working toward master's degrees can complete requirements for degrees in elementary education and social work at that campus. Although established as a campus strictly for commuting students, Mansfield now offers a residential option. Students who want to experience living on campus may choose to live in a new student-housing community located within walking distance of the campus.

Where both Middletown and Mansfield differ from most community colleges is that they are part of the Miami University and The Ohio State University systems, respectively. Course offerings are determined by committees in Oxford and Columbus, and faculty are members of their home departments on the main campus; promotion and tenure decisions are made in Oxford and Columbus, and faculty are tenured to the university not to the individual campus. Perhaps, then, the most distinctive difference between teaching at a branch campus and teaching at a community college is the faculty's affiliation to a discipline. The separation from a professional (such as English) discipline experienced by community-college faculty (McGrath & Spear 1991; Ratliff 1992) is one that would be professionally suicidal for branch-campus faculty, given that the first decision-making level for all promotion and tenure candidates is within the home department. To isolate oneself from one's department would make it extremely difficult to receive a favorable judgment, hence English faculty at Middletown and Mansfield make a concerted effort to be active members of their home departments in Oxford and Columbus.

But how did we get here? And, where is "here?"

Jeff

My story begins in graduate school in the mid-1970s. From the outset, I was not following what Cynthia Tuell calls the "'normal progression'" (1993, 127) of teaching assistant for several years and then assistant professor on a tenure track. After completing my M.A., I found part-time work teaching composition at two local four-year institutions while continuing coursework toward my Ph.D. My plans were to complete a degree in Victorian literature, locate a full-time literature position at a four-year college, and follow the "normal progression." However, economic circumstances intervened, and I was glad to assume my first full-time teaching position while still writing my dissertation. That position took me several hundred miles away to a community college in western Maryland where I taught a variety of composition courses and discovered that teaching at a community college was quite rewarding because of the heterogeneous student body whose diverse levels of preparation and varied ages presented stimulating teaching challenges. However, the position was one I viewed from the outset as a detour while I finished my degree.

At the end of my three years at the community college, two important events occurred: (1) I wrote my first article for publication, a practical pedagogical piece that subsequently appeared in *Teaching English in the Two-Year College* in 1979. (2) I found a full-time position as an instructor at a four-year campus in Cincinnati, Ohio. My level of awareness of how I fit into the profession was rather limited in those days. I had already been marginalized in a number of ways without being particularly conscious of it: as a part-time faculty member in New York, as a community-college teacher in Maryland, and now as an instructor in Cincinnati. My job was described officially as a "terminal position," meaning that after my three-year contract expired, so did I, at least professionally. I finished my dissertation in only two years and I went back into the job market. But something had happened during those two years. I decided that I wanted to go back to a two-year campus. I missed the challenges and the variety of students, but I also had had a taste of the elitism of the four-year college.

When George Vaughan talks about the myth of scholarship at four-year campuses, his words ring true to my experience. Vaughan is not disparaging the notion of scholarship; however, he critiques the idea that all four-year faculty are scholars and researchers, terming that a myth (1992, 25). During my two years at the four-year campus, I became quite frightened by this myth, and I do not think I recognized that it was a myth. Talk in the hallways was always about publishing; in retrospect, I think that there was more talk than action, but the talk was intimidating. When one of the faculty was quoted in the publicity for a new textbook, the joke that made the rounds was that he needed to list the one-sentence blurb in his annual service report as a publication. I was intimidated because I had no clear sense of how I could publish enough to avoid perishing. My strengths, although acknowledged by the department, were in the classroom as a teacher, and my publishing future seemed shaky to me, at best.

Thus, I leaped at the opportunity to apply for a position at one of Miami's two-year campuses. The employment screening process itself was instructive, although I did not learn the lessons well until later. I drove the thirty miles from my home to Oxford to begin my interviews with the department's search committee. After morning meetings with the committee, the department chair, and the Dean of Arts and Science, it was time for me to visit the Middletown campus. It was also midday, but lunch was not on the agenda. I was given a road map by the department chair with instructions about how to find my way to the branch campus. I was also given several record albums he had borrowed from a member of the English Department at Middletown and asked to return them. At Middletown, I met with the five members of the department, an interview that went very well because I drew on my experiences at the community college and made a connection with the faculty whose teaching experiences had been similar to mine.

Continuing the interview process, I met with the Executive Director of the campus, a position that I was assured was equivalent to a deanship (although the title of "Dean" is still not accorded the position two decades later). It is a commonplace to note that community-college faculty have much in common with high-school teachers and, historically, many of the first community-college faculty were drawn from the ranks of high-school teachers. In this case, the campus Executive Director was a former high-school principal and school superintendent. My most vivid recollection of that interview was how insistent he was that the position for which I was interviewing was at the two-year campus and that it would not and could not be a stepping-stone to a position at the four-year campus. I was equally insistent that I not only understood but actually preferred to be at the branch campus. He had looked at my record-Ph.D. in literature from an eastern university, two publications (by this time, I had written an informal piece on *Huckleberry Finn* and published it in a nonrefereed journal), and recent employment history, and determined that I was probably not serious about a permanent position at a two-year campus.

At that time, we both apparently accepted the standard image of the two-year campus as a "lesser" place to work. He saw me in the elevator pressing buttons to the penthouse or at least to Kysar's fourth floor; I saw myself as unwilling to press those higher buttons because of some fear that I might not be able to succeed at higher altitudes. Several commentators have noted that two-year faculty members are complicit to some extent in the devalued position they hold (Dziech & Vilter 1992, 4; Vaughan 1992, 24); I was certainly complicit at that time.

Karen

While a graduate student in composition and rhetoric at a four-year research institution during an era when postmodern theories predominated, I was beleaguered by questions of location—theoretical, social, and geographic. Now, as a new assistant professor, I continue to read about, write about, discuss, argue, or generally contemplate how those questions infiltrate every facet of my developing professional identity. At times, I wonder if I have fixated on the question of theoretical location because I expend so much time and energy shaping and reshaping, even agonizing over, my particular theoretical position. I imagine my attention to theory is not surprising, especially at this social and historical moment when composition is in the midst of contentious debates about its very definition and purpose as a discipline. I've noticed, though, that since I taught composition, composition and literature, and women's studies courses at the Middletown campus and developmental reading and writing, composition, and rhetorical theory at the Mansfield campus, the questions I've been asking about my theoretical location have become more intricately intertwined with my own and my students' social and geographic locations. Just when I think I've figured out "where I am," at least in theoretical terms, my triple branch-campus experience—first as a nontraditional student and then as an instructor at Middletown, and now as an assistant professor at Mansfield—intervenes to complicate my training at a major research university.

A glance at my years in graduate school suggests a traditional climb toward a career as an academic. In most ways—except perhaps for my status as an older, returning student—I've followed Tuell's "normal progression'" to the letter. I served as a graduate assistant for two years while completing my master's in composition and rhetoric, and as a teaching assistant for four years of my Ph.D. program. I spent a fifth year as a dissertation scholar at Miami, finishing the project during another year as a part-time adjunct professor. My graduate-school years initiated me into the academic discourse community of my four-year research institution while I taught courses in composition, composition and literature, advanced college composition, composition and theory and pedagogy for new graduate student teachers, and workshops for K–12 teachers in the Ohio Writing Project. The theoretical orientation I claim has also been influenced by the administrative work I undertook as Assistant Director of College Composition, by the stances I took on issues debated by departmental committees, by the topics I've chosen to address at professional conferences, and by the arguments I've made in seminar papers and in publications such as a collaborative piece about feminist pedagogy published in *College Composition and Communication.* Overall, my activities as a graduate student at Miami have allowed me to begin systematically establishing an identity as a professional in composition at a four-year research institution.

But, with the Ph.D. now finished, that's not where I am. When I began to scan the MLA Joblist in search of a permanent job, I realized that my connections with the branch campus have left cultural and intellectual legacies. Those connections have profoundly influenced who I am and where I want to be—on the tenure track at a regional campus of a major research institution. The route I took to arrive at exactly that type of position at The Ohio State University at Mansfield was somewhat circuitous, however. For example, the reading list I compiled for my comprehensive examination appears fairly traditional with its theoretical slant and its careful inclusion of both canonical and noncanonical texts. The list also delineates an overarching focus on the social contexts of the teaching of language, an interest perhaps expected from someone intimately familiar with disenfranchised segments of the population. I chose composition and rhetoric and sociolinguistics as my two majors because both have recently offered intense critiques of knowledge-making as a politically neutral process, and both have given long overdue attention to institutionalized social inequalities.

What wasn't on my list also points to a break with tradition. Rather than declare a major in literature, I devised a second major in sociolinguistics. I chose that route for a couple of reasons. First, even though I had completed more graduate courses in literature than in sociolinguistics, I confronted an elitism in many of my literature courses that I never imagined as an enthusiastic undergraduate literature major on a branch campus. One particularly vivid memory places me around a seminar table in an American literature course. I am the only compositionist in the class of nearly twenty students, and I am the one the instructor singles out as most complicit in what she terms "the oppressive machine." She stands behind my chair as she alternately excoriates compositionists for dutifully training students to take their places within capitalism and praises aspiring literary scholars for exposing and rejecting this corrupt system. An equally nightmarish memory places me in a professor's office. Although I have carefully written and rewritten and rewritten my seminar paper for his course in literary theory, he tells me that my work will remain in the B range until I "admit that feminists have backed themselves into a corner," until I figure out that feminist theory is not a viable scholarly approach to understanding a piece of literature. As I turn to leave, he assures me that I am "bright enough to figure it out." Although I continue to enjoy reading, discussing, teaching, and writing about literature, these graduate experiences convince me that there was no place for me in that particular academic discourse community.

My second reason for choosing sociolinguistics as my second major hinged on the fact that it is, like composition and rhetoric, my first major, and anthropology, my cognate field, an applied discipline. By that, I mean that the field overtly declares social change as one of its primary objectives. Many contemporary sociolinguists confront theoretical questions of ideology, representation, discourse, power, and subjectivity in an openly political manner that goes beyond descriptive accounts of the production, internal structure, and organization of texts. Their aim is twofold: They study language and society as entities that cannot be separated and they consider language not as an innocent medium but as a practice that contributes to social inequalities.

Like my reading list, my dissertation and the book based on that project that I am currently writing seem to position me squarely within a research university. Solidly grounded in rhetorical theory and history and more theoretical than pedagogical, my research focuses on environmental rhetoric, particularly in terms of how language is used to constitute the social and natural worlds. I'm interested in various genres of texts about the natural environment because they are cultural sites where convergences of political, economic, aesthetic, ethical, and scientific issues can be analyzed from a rhetorical perspective. Although my project may seem far removed from the classroom, it has much to do with the way I teach composition, as a rhetorical engagement with questions of language and power. Like my composition courses, it concerns the cultural work language does and the consequences for disenfranchised groups of people. As I transform my dissertation into a book manuscript, I am sharpening my analysis and critique of environmental policy to show how this discourse works on local and global levels, not just to reflect social inequalities but to construct them. I intend this interwoven history of rhetoric(s) and environmentalism(s) not as just another intellectual reappraisal of the various relations between humans and nature but also as an appeal to consider how unequal relations between different cultural groups are maintained with language and in the name of nature.

While I was in graduate school, I worked to develop a foundation from which to teach, do research, and write, and I had in the back of my mind the goal of returning to my two-year campus roots when I finished my doctorate. It seemed to me an ideal place for someone like me who aligns herself with theorists such as Patricia Harkin and John Schilb who see composition as "not merely the service component of the English Department but also an inquiry into cultural values" (1991, 1). I was thinking primarily of branch-campus students when I stated in the rationale I wrote for the composition-and-rhetoric portion of my reading list:

> The social construction paradigm most influences my teaching because of its emphasis on the social dimensions of the writing process and its concomitant dedication to achieving a literate democracy. What that theoretical position means for my students, my research, and my writing is that we question the boundaries between disciplines and genres; that we consider how cultural work is conducted with language; that we examine how the personal is bound up with the social; that we attend to ways our readings and writings affect not only our classroom community, but communities outside the academy; and that we explore and critique contexts for knowledge with the aim of fostering our sense of social responsibility.

Such goals for writing courses are imperative at places like the Middletown campus and the Mansfield campus, geographic sites that look much like the ubiquitous community college Ira Shor describes with its "giant parking lots surrounding drab buildings, computer registration and mass counseling, fiberglass furniture jammed against cinderblock walls, classes crowded into tight block scheduling to maximize use of time, space, and personnel, and the inevitable flourescent-formica cafeteria . . . " (1987, 12–13). In fact, the goals I have for my writing courses take on a material reality that I couldn't begin to achieve when I taught courses based on the same goals in Oxford where its signature red-brick Georgian architecture, formal gardens, and tolling Beta Bells mark it as a "public ivy."

Jeff

As I began teaching at the branch campus, I still considered myself a literature teacher who was also interested in composition, somehow ignoring the fact that literature was not central to the mission of my new campus (Alford &

Kroll 1997, 58). Gradually, I fell into composition and rhetoric and began to write about it. That decision was determined in large part by where I was. Although my teaching load included one introductory literature course per term, my primary assignment was teaching three to four classes of composition every term, plus two to three more sections in the summer. From a practical standpoint, however, it made sense for me to move into composition as well because the composition faculty on the main campus welcomed my interest while the literature faculty continued to treat me as invisible.

Invisible is a word that keeps coming up as I read about two-year college faculty. Alford and Kroll use that adjective to describe the place of community-college faculty in the history of composition studies (1997, 59). Nancy La-Paglia's study of how two-year colleges are treated in American fiction concludes that "the two-year college teacher is almost invisible in American fiction" (1994, 103). My invisibility to my literature colleagues was understandable: They literally did not see me on a daily basis because I taught twenty-five miles away. I was seen briefly for awhile by a colleague who read one of the two articles that I published on Victorian literature out of my dissertation, but, for the most part, my work was so different from theirs that we had no point of contact. I not only taught mostly writing courses, but, when I did teach literature, I taught it to non-English majors. I never encountered large numbers of English majors in my classes or taught any graduate students. My working conditions were not conducive to keeping up with the Victorian literature I had once studied, particularly given my academic isolation.

However, the composition faculty on the main campus welcomed my participation in their regular meetings to discuss pedagogy and theory and research interests. Melissa Sue Kort tells her story of returning to a four-year institution to pursue a doctorate in literature after many years of teaching at a community college and notes that one of the difficulties she had fitting into the new department was the "nasty sibling rivalry" (1994, 177) between literature and composition. That rivalry was not necessarily a nasty one at Miami at the time I joined the faculty, but the composition group certainly had more to gain by adding to its number than did the literature group.

As those first few years went by, I accomplished enough to become more visible. At least my colleagues knew me by sight and sometimes by my work on committees or by my professional activities as listed in the university's in-house newsletter. What did they think of me? One colleague, a very traditional literature professor, intended a compliment when he said to me, in a tone of commiseration, "Are you sure there's no way for you to get a transfer over here to Oxford?" I heard the echoes of my job interview in that question. My response was to tell him that I was not looking for a transfer because I quite enjoyed my position at the branch campus. He looked either stunned or perhaps merely skeptical. Clearly, he embraced the attitude that Kort reported when she returned to graduate school: "Some of my fellow students . . . seemed to consider two-year college teaching only as a mark of some failure to 'make it'" (1994, 181).

Dziech and Vilter focus on elitism in the introduction to their collection of essays:

> When one spends a quarter of a century working in a two-year college that is part of one of the nation's largest universities, concerns about status inevitably arise. At the University of Cincinnati's University College, the struggle for recognition and respect can be a daily fact of life; and, occasionally, on bad days, it has occurred to both of us that we are, in a very real sense, prisoners of elitism. At those times, whether we, in University College, are better or worse off than our colleagues in community colleges geographically distant from the benefits of a large university seems less important to us than whether or not our colleagues across campus understand our mission and value our contributions to scholarship and teaching. (1992, 1)

That elitism is based primarily on the prestige attached to research versus the devalued position of teaching. In a special issue of *Teaching English in the Two-Year College (TETYC)*, titled "Celebrating the Two-Year College," Clyde Muse, president of a community college, noted that the community college "does not focus on adding to the research base but rather focuses on using the available research base to meet local needs" (1990, 76). Looking more closely at that special issue, it is hard not to acknowledge the validity of Muse's description. There are seven substantial articles in that issue, not counting the shorter response pieces and instructional notes. Of those seven, three have no bibliographical references. The four articles that do provide bibliographical references list forty-one sources; only two of the forty-one articles were previously published in *TETYC*. Looking at the March 1999 issue, nine years later, we find seven articles of substance, six with lists of sources. The fifty-four sources cited include five references to articles published in *TETYC*, all five appearing in the same article. The knowledge base Muse speaks about is not one being built by contributors to *TETYC* it would seem.

In the May 1990 issue of *TETYC*, not much more than twenty-five pages after Muse's remarks, Keith Kroll argues that "community building must occur beyond the classroom: community-college faculty, including English faculty, must establish a professional identity within the academic community of higher education. . . . It is a lack of 'knowledge-making' and a resulting lack of professional identity that have engendered . . . [an] anti-intellectual environment and faculty burnout" at two-year colleges (1992, 103). Kroll continues his argument by noting the historical separation of teaching and scholarship and observing that "faculty who do write and publish often face hostility from administrators and other faculty" (1990, 106). McGrath and Spear make a similar argument that two-year faculty whose commitment to publication is to publicly face criticism from their community-college peers (1991, 140). Indeed, after I had started to publish articles, one of my Middletown colleagues expressed surprise when I spoke of my anticipated teaching assignment; he said that he had expected me to be maneuvering for a transfer to the main campus. The inference I drew was that in his eyes the four-year campus is where I belonged.

To McGrath and Spear the consequences of this separation of teaching and scholarship is that two-year faculty have created a practitioners' culture, borrowing the concept from Stephen North's (1987) examination of how knowledge is made in composition (an interesting and significant borrowing because McGrath and Spear are not writing only about English faculty). In their view, that practitioners' culture is anti-intellectual as well as being an oral culture with a decided bias against communicating ideas in print, preferring instead to "share" through experiential, oral narratives (McGrath & Spear 1991, 148–54). Ratliff, in his comments on how teaching has been separated from specific disciplines, argues that "academic disciplines play a vital role in scholarly inquiry" and urges that good teaching requires knowledge of a discipline (1992, 44).

Vaughan wants to rehabilitate the image of the two-year college faculty member by redefining scholarship in a way that matches the mission of the community college. He sketches a portrait of the community-college teacher who sets up a binary opposition between research and teaching, opting to make the "good and true" choice of being a teacher (1994, 213). But Vaughan wants to connect teaching and scholarship, which he defines as "the systematic pursuit of a topic, an objective, rational inquiry requiring critical analysis . . . [that] results in a product that is shared with others and that is subject to the criticism of individuals qualified to judge the product" (1994, 216). Tuell makes a shrewd observation about the products of scholarship when she notes that "publications do have tangible substances; real ink on real paper in real books and journals, enjoying lifelong citation on curriculum vitae. But such substantiality cannot be claimed for teaching" (1993, 131).

The point is that by choosing, often in an aggressive, even hostile manner, to define ourselves as "teachers" in opposition to "researchers" at four-year campuses, figures who may seem threatening to us (Tuell 1993, 140), we assign ourselves to a position perceived as inferior. That position is compounded by our choice of the word "teacher." McGrath and Spear note that community-college faculty refer to themselves as "teachers" as high school faculty do while four-year faculty tend to use the word "instructor" instead (1991, 140). As I worked on a college-level textbook with a colleague, we consciously chose to use the word "teacher" in the manuscript because our target readership was the two-year college faculty member. Our copy editor as a matter of course switched all of those references to "instructor," revealing her own biases.

Karen

Both my Middletown and Mansfield students have told me that the process-oriented, social-constructionist theory that undergirds my pedagogy fits well with their particular social and geographic locations. They're relieved when I tell them that we won't be focusing on grammar or mechanics until near the end of the course when they will polish those pieces chosen for their portfolios, that I won't lecture but will expect them to carry the responsibility for discussions, and that I don't expect all of us to glean the same meanings from texts. Most of them are undaunted when I present them with the same syllabi taught on the main campuses, and many of them produce more interesting, if less superficially flawless, writing than their main-campus counterparts. I've achieved some measure of success, I believe, when the issues we discuss in class and write about are integrated into our public and private lives. Two particularly telling examples come to mind. One of my colleagues at the Middletown campus shared with me a discourse analysis paper that had been collaboratively written by several of her students. The paper focused on a conversation they had witnessed among my students. In this impromptu conversation, my students revisited and interrogated our debate about standard English. These students returned to the issue on their own, outside the classroom, in that "flourescent-formica" cafeteria called "The Commons" at Middletown. Equally revealing is the message one of my Mansfield students posted on our listserv concerning her recent change of heart about homosexuals. She thanks her classmates and me for our discussions about language and sociocultural difference because they have led her to reconsider her denunciation of a friend who recently revealed his sexual orientation to her.

As I think about it from my new position as assistant professor, I understand that the branch-campus students at Miami were not just the primary reason but perhaps the only reason I sought a job at a branch campus as a permanent place. One incident stands out and is, in fact, one of the main reasons that I taught the standard syllabus as it was designed by the first-year writing program at Oxford. As a junior English major, I remember vividly my own feelings of disappointment—and inadequacy—when I casually asked the instructor of an upper-level literature course why we were reading so few books and writing so few papers. She read my question as a complaint and reminded me that I was a branch-campus student taking a branch-campus course. In other words, it was impertinent of me to expect a course as rigorous as one I might take if I were a main-campus student.

Years later, I realize that this instructor and I would agree that composition and literature are intensely local constructions and must reflect, both theoretically and pedagogically, the social and geographic spaces that shape them. We just disagree—vehemently disagree—about how social and geographic locations should figure into our theories and practices. While I expect classroom activities to play out differently in two very different places like Oxford and Middletown or Columbus and Mansfield, it is patently unfair to automatically expect less from branch-campus students just because they are branch-campus students. I remain disturbed by this incident all of these years later because it is clear that this instructor saw her students not only as different but also as inferior. Too many main-campus instructors also underestimate their students' abilities and even talk about students as if they don't like them, but I wonder if this construction of students isn't more pervasive on branch campuses. The time I've spent at Mansfield is too short for me to know how well I will cope if that is indeed so.

Perhaps incidents like this one, although thankfully few, should have rendered me somewhat immune to the "culture shock that many writing teachers find when they leave the safe haven of graduate school for teaching positions in the two-year college" (Alford & Kroll 1997, 60). But I was shocked when, as I prepared to teach for the first time on the branch campus, Donald Greive's *A Handbook for Adjunct/Part-Time Faculty and Teachers of Adults* appeared in my mailbox. I eagerly scanned it, expecting articles about issues such as teaching nontraditional students, designing syllabi that accommodate and celebrate a plurality of literacies, and managing research and publication in addition to a heavy teaching load. Although the guide does offer a chapter titled "Teaching Adult Students," Greive seems to want to assure instructors that adult students are pretty much like every other student, in every other educational institution, in every other region. He relies on a generic model to describe "the students" and explains that the chapter is "intended to provide a better understanding of today's students" (1990, 51). Although Greive apparently considers some kind of historical perspective important to his profile of "today's students," he doesn't offer specifics but casts them en masse as "more demanding," "more interesting," and "more challenging" (52).

To be fair, I should mention that Greive's guide does recognize the changing look of educational institutions and notes the "multicultural and multilingual student body" (1990, 1) typical of classrooms in the 1990s. Yet Greive's understanding of diversity seems not only disappointingly shallow but blatantly ethnocentric. He sees the "multicultural and multilingual student body" as an "influx," a term that carries a negative connotation, while, only three pages later, he posits a list of qualities of good teaching, which includes "understanding our culture" (1990, 4). I remember wondering just whose culture he meant and how that "multicultural and multilingual student body" might respond to a teacher who possessed no awareness of the problem of erasing minority cultures by lumping them under "our culture." I also remember wondering if a guide intended for anyone other than "adjunct/part-time" faculty would caution instructors to appear "neat and professional," especially "if one has a tendency toward casual or even sloppy appearance" (1990, 5).

I might have disregarded Greive except that during the semesters I taught at the branch campus, I encountered other teachers who seemed to adopt and perpetuate his views. While I knew at least two branch-campus instructors who understood and supported my approach to teaching composition, I rarely saw them because they both taught on days I didn't. The result was an intellectual isolation as enervating as I ever hope to know. It seemed that the only colleagues I happened to encounter complained about two aspects of their jobs: (1) the inferior students they were expected to teach or (2) other teachers (like me) who failed to stress the "basics" of a writing course, leaving their students ignorant of where to place commas on their in-class essay exams. I sensed a pervasive disapproval of my theoretical objective to define a writing class as something more than a place for students to develop job skills and an attitude appropriate for menial work. Particularly illustrative is one administrator's obvious discomfort during a faculty-development workshop where I gave a presentation on the importance of recognizing gendered codes of behavior in the classroom. Missing the point of my talk altogether, he mentioned that he'd had few complaints from students until instructors brought issues of race, class, and gender into the classroom.

Jeff

I began to move into scholarship not long after affiliating with the composition faculty at Miami, but my move was a very self-conscious and tentative one, born of my embracing the myth of research that Vaughan (1994) describes. In LaPaglia's study of community-college faculty, she quotes one faculty member who says, "I'm no more than a closet scholar, but a master teacher . . . " (1994, 128). That self-deprecatory label describes my first endeavors to publish in composition. In my fourth year at Middletown, I submitted an article to *English in the Two-Year College,* a newsletter that has since ceased publication. "The 'Paradigm Shift' in Composition Instruction: Are Our Students Shifting with Us?" began rather hesitantly as if I were unsure of my right to speak because my essay was not hard-core research. Here is the opening paragraph of that essay:

> I have no empirical evidence to offer in the following essay. Well, actually, I do, but I freely acknowledge that it is likely to be viewed as too scant or as not statistically valid. But I am interested instead in describing a gut reaction, a feeling that I have about the current crop of freshmen in our composition classrooms: they are, in significant numbers, more traditional about writing instruction than we are. Let me amplify on that statement by explaining its genesis. (1)
>
> I expect to continue to experiment in my classes, perhaps not in any empirical or controlled manner, but in the time-honored manner of the two-year campus. As we look ahead to the future of the two-year college, I urge that we continue to read the journals, attend the conferences, and think about implementing the new ideas and techniques which sound most convincingly useful to writing instruction. We face roomfuls of students who are waiting for us to be innovative, who want us to be innovative. Let us make certain that we take advantage of our special opportunity to help evolve more effective ways to teach writing. (1985, 4–5)

Actually, the essay was based on more than the "gut reaction" mentioned in the introduction: I had administered and analyzed a valid and respected attitudinal survey to my students. My hesitation, however, reveals much about how I positioned myself as a scholar at that time.

Almost two decades later, after tenure and two promotions, I reject the notion of being a closet scholar. My scholarship may not look traditional for a professor or even for a compositionist, but it is scholarship by Vaughan's standards or by Kroll's criteria for classroom research. I define myself simply as a teacher-scholar. Another anecdote illustrates the change in my position. After submitting a chapter to an editor for inclusion in an upcoming collection of essays, I received his response. He questioned whether my argument was really focused on two-year campuses and suggested opening up the discussion because many basic writers attend other kinds of institutions. I revised the piece and wrote back to him as follows:

> I read your comments and suggestions carefully. Let me preview for you what I've worked on here. I have attempted to make clear that my ideas are not necessarily useful only at the two-year campus, but that they are particularly well-suited for that location. I don't know whether my explicit discussion of this issue at the end of the piece will work for you; I'm sure you'll let me know. Quite frankly, this is at least partly a political issue for me. I'm not familiar with all the contributors you have listed in the book, but I haven't seen any names that suggest to me a two-year campus focus. I'd like to see the book acknowledge two-year campuses explicitly; I can see your point that much or even all of what I discuss here is relevant at any college campus. But to me there's still a difference about the two-year campuses and their students that informs the piece, so I've tried to preserve that difference.

At this point in my career I know where I am: at a two-year campus that is part of a four-year university. I must function—and I want to function—as community-college teachers do by marrying scholarship with teaching, but that is at least in part due to my affiliation with a four-year campus, which has pushed me all along to be "scholarly" in some fashion.[1] But that makes me different from community-college faculty described in the literature as well as in my own experience.

At a major conference for composition teachers, researchers, and scholars, I attended a workshop for two-year college teachers. As part of a small group focused on faculty development, I asked the group at one point whether they felt any sense of discomfort at the conference, any sense of not being entirely welcome. I asked because I had noticed that most of the sessions in which I participated were attended by either four-year or two-year faculty but rarely by a mixed group. I was eager to engage in a discussion of our experiences and perceptions, but what I encountered was silence. No one in my small group had anything at all to say. I still do not know how to read that silence: Was it denial? Was I so wrong in my perceptions that they were stunned? Had I broken some taboo by asking such a question?

The experience reminded me of an unsettling situation with my publisher. A colleague and I were writing a college reader under the working title of *The Two-Year College Reader.* As part of the review process, readers were asked their opinion of the book's projected title. The responses were illuminating:

I don't like the title at all. It's flat and uninteresting—which the text certainly isn't. Besides that, the two-year is going to block off part of the market (at least I can see an instructor at a four-year school scanning catalogs and sliding right past this title). Change the title, please.

As the authors may already suspect, a text entitled *The Two-Year College Reader* would be a "tough sell" at [our campus]. Our students would have no objection, but our faculty, who select texts, would. Nancy LaPaglia . . . is on target in her description of the low esteem in which two-year colleges are held, particularly in large urban areas. Our campus coexists with [several four-year campuses in the area]. We would be reluctant to choose a text that [implies] a "difference."

The choice of title is a bit sticky, of course, because of the term "two-year college." I say use it. The majority of students enrolled in composition courses are in two-year colleges, and the textbook authors gear the book specifically to this audience whom they know first-hand. While I can visualize Joe Blow at XYZ University not bothering to examine the book because of the title, I can visualize even more teachers in the two-year programs giving it an edge to start with, thinking "At long last, authors and publishers are recognizing the distinctive characteristics of two-year college populations."

The second reviewer notes the low esteem in which the two-year campus is held but seems not to have noticed that he himself has accepted that image. The publisher had become increasingly skittish about the title, so my colleague and I sent the following response:

The market for our book is the two-year college faculty member who attends conferences and reads professional journals and keeps up with recent developments in the field. NCTE published a collection of essays, *Two-Year College English: Essays for a New Century* edited by Mark Reynolds; Boynton/Cook is at work on *The Politics of Writing in the Two-Year College* as a companion to the award-winning *The Politics of Writing Instruction* by Bullock and Trimbur (1991). Clearly, an audience exists already of well-informed two-year college faculty. They are the ones we hope to reach. We agree that *The Two-Year College Reader* is a title that will most likely not sell at any four-year colleges, but that is a secondary market at best for this book. We are genuinely convinced that this book is a reader for the two-year college students in fundamentally significant ways that no other book can match; we'd like a title that declares that significance overtly.

This story is instructive in what it says about the uphill battle facing two-year college faculty as they struggle to define who they are while acknowledging where they are. The publisher, not surprisingly, changed the title of the book; the only surprise was that it took over a year for it to happen. The message is that "four-year" is the normative adjective when describing college. Although we changed our book's title, we did not change it to *The Four-Year College*

Reader. However, the only way to become visible as a two-year college faculty member is by virtue of the adjective "two-year." Hence, the community-college teacher's journal is *Teaching English in the Two-Year College,* while a comparable journal for four-year college instructors (and anyone else who wishes to read it) is simply the *Journal of Teaching Writing.* "Four-year" remains the default position, and identifying our book as *The Two-Year College Reader* marked it as clearly different, and, in marketing terms, inferior.

Karen

After teaching a number of courses on the branch campus, I remained discomfited by the attitudes of some of my colleagues there. I couldn't rely on my course work to guide me because not one of my many graduate courses in composition, rhetoric, sociolinguistics, or literature dealt in any direct or sustained way with teaching composition on a two-year campus. I suspect, though, that I may be better off than many other graduate students who are interested in two-year campuses because I worked with a number of faculty members whose political agenda is to situate composition by challenging universalized, ahistorical, and decontextualized notions of literacy. In fact, the standard composition syllabus at Miami addressed issues particularly relevant to two-year campuses because it understood literacy as a set of encoded values — social, cultural, political, historical, and economic values that disempower more often than they empower. As Alford and Kroll point out, two-year campuses seem to be invisible in that "little of the important work in composition has considered the differences between two- and four-year institutions" (1997, 60). Unfortunately, the same seems to be true of graduate programs in composition.

Even though I am now on the tenure track, I continue to struggle to find my niche in the profession. I continue to struggle to reconcile my differences as a nontraditional student from a branch campus with my traditional progression as an academic. For most of my graduate career, the answer has seemed simple. I'd just tuck my passionately held theoretical position under my arm and take it to the geographical and social place with which I'm most comfortable: the two-year campus. But even though I have done exactly that, I'm still not sure how I fit there. Before I took the job at Ohio State, I was troubled by the binary opposition between teaching and research that seems to hang over two-year campuses. While I've never intended to follow the model that defines an academic as someone who teaches solely to support her research, I've never considered teaching without participating in a community that publishes scholarly work. Instead, I've worried about how I would manage to write and publish and teach the heavy course load typical of two-year campus faculty all at the same time.

As it turns out, my worries were groundless, or so it seems. In my new position as assistant professor at Mansfield, I am heartened to find that what the chair told me during my interview seems to have some measure of truth to it. He explained that I would be a member of the Department of English at The

Ohio State University, with attendant rights and responsibilities. I would just happen to teach at the campus in Mansfield. He was very careful not to use typical exclusionary language such as "branch/regional campus" and "main campus" when he informed me that I would have essentially the same teaching load and the same research opportunities as my Columbus colleagues. He stressed that promotion and tenure decisions would be made with no regard for my primary campus affiliation.

My thus far brief experience at Mansfield has only added to my perplexity about the image of the two-year campus, particularly the image of faculty who are viewed as "different and less as instructors, teaching in a less-desirable location, and working with less-prepared students," as we wrote at the beginning of this essay. While I was a graduate student who was often identified as a two-year campus student/scholar/teacher, I've experienced a positive response to that locatedness, a response that seems unusual. Perhaps that's because my branch-campus teaching worked to differentiate me from the other graduate students in my large department. Typical of most graduate programs, M.A. and Ph.D. students in my department rarely had the opportunity to teach any course other than the two-semester composition sequence on the main campus. The economic reality is that there are at least 120 sections of those courses to staff every semester. So being assigned to teach on one of the branch campuses was a marker of seniority and prestige. Because I've taught a number of composition and composition and literature, as well as a women's studies course at the Middletown campus, my difference as a branch-campus teacher evolved into a unique professional characteristic. That characteristic is often referred to as a marker of my expertise as a teacher and was mentioned in the two teaching awards I've won, as well as in the announcement of my appointment to the position as Assistant Director of College Composition. My affiliation with two-year college teaching as a graduate student seems to have been seen in a much more positive light than Kort and others report—and I'm left wondering why.

I can think of at least two reasons, the first more encouraging than the second. Perhaps an appreciation of my participation in a marginalized community portended positive change in that it reflects composition's recent attention to less-powerful and long-silenced voices. Many of the conversations, theoretical as well as practical, that went on in the halls and offices of Bachelor Hall, the home of the Oxford campus English Department, had to do with teaching writing. Many of us teach the standard syllabus that explicitly stated in *College Composition at Miami,* the handbook for first-year composition students, that the fundamental assumption underlying the syllabus was that "language constructs social difference in all spheres of discourse" (Aschauer 1972, 15). I think that my colleagues ask me about intersections between the syllabus and my differently located branch-campus students because I could situate our theoretical inquiry in a different place and offer an otherwise unrepresented view.

Another possible explanation is less optimistic. Perhaps I was positively instead of negatively marked by my branch-campus teaching experience because

I was not permanently located there. Who I was as a composition instructor was not so rigidly defined by where I was because my stay at the branch campus, just as my stay at the main campus, was temporary. My commitment to the branch campus was seen as a willingness to broaden and enrich my teaching experience at that moment in my career when I was not tied to any particular location instead of as a failure to succeed in a more prestigious position. I was never entirely or inescapably a member of the two-year campus because I was either teaching a course on the main campus at the same time I was teaching on the branch campus, or I was expected to return to the main campus in the near future.

Jeff

As I conclude my part of this narrative, I'm drawn back to Bambara's Miss Moore, whose astute observations nevertheless are never actively turned back on herself. Does she herself acknowledge that *where* she is is *who* she is? Or, doesn't it have to be that way for her either? Her putative students sneer at her, tolerate her, try to ignore her. As the story's narrator reports, the other adults in the community ridicule and complain about her behind her back even while turning their children over to her. Miss Moore exists in a vacuum, isolated from other teachers, the other adults, the young people she tries to teach. She, like Karen, has returned to her roots, the place she came from, and while no one in the story expends much energy puzzling out why she would do so, my students at Middletown are often surprised, even aghast, that she would go back. Through it all, however, Miss Moore pursues her intentions of teaching young people lessons that may assist them to understand where they are located and what the implications of their location might be.

There's something admirable, almost heroic about Miss Moore, and that's the point at which I want to drop the analogy because there's nothing heroic about working at a two-year branch campus. It is a good job, an important job, no better or worse than teaching anywhere else. But, as writing this essay has helped me to learn, it is also not like teaching anywhere else, either. So I know where I am professionally, I think, and I can trace the journey that brought me here, but which button on Kysar's metaphorical elevator I actually pressed to get to this location is something of a mystery to me, more a case of knowing which ones I didn't press than recalling the precise one I did.

Karen

Even though I am now an assistant professor who is working toward tenure from my chosen place on a regional campus, questions of location are no less complex, no less personal or political, no less pressing than they were when, as a graduate student, I could only imagine where "here" might be. For me, the elevator doors recently opened. I stepped on, scanned the buttons, and pushed one (not without trepidation) that delivered me to a place somewhere between the community college and the research university. It seems I've left behind one complex relationship between two-year and four-year campuses to grapple with another. In my new position, one large question about location predominates: To what extent does where I am determine who I am? I can answer only tentatively. Strictly speaking, I am a faculty member at The Ohio State University who teaches on the Mansfield campus. But not so strictly speaking, I am a faculty member on a branch campus. Although I have essentially the same annual teaching load as my Columbus colleagues, I teach 2/2/2 load, while they teach 2/2/1. That is, I teach one additional class each year compared to my Columbus colleagues. The argument is that branch-campus classes are smaller, so we end up teaching the same number of students. I teach a broader range of courses, from a 100-level developmental writing to a 500-level rhetorical theory, and my guess is that I teach more lower-division, labor-intensive writing courses than do my Columbus counterparts. Only recently, the chair proposed a new tenure and promotion plan that would separate the regional-campuses from Columbus, a plan that has been met with intense opposition from most regional-campus faculty, a plan that I feel could not help but define me as somehow different and less as an instructor and scholar. Yet despite the tensions between two-year and four-year campuses, I think that this theoretical, social, and geographic place will prove most conducive to my continuing development as a professional in composition and rhetoric. I'm almost convinced by one of my colleagues at Mansfield who tells me that, because of where we are, "We have the best of both worlds." But I can't yet say for sure.

Jeff

When we began this essay, we asserted that it would not end in a nice, neat package, but that it would trail off. As I read what we have written, the image of the elevator smacks to me of the well-made tale; it provides an apt analogy that has proven irresistible and lends a sense of closure to the piece that I know I had not expected to reach. But, as I put the finishing touches on what I thought was the final, final edited draft, I was struck forcefully by something I had missed somehow during the time that we have worked on this paper. Have I ever written anything for publication that says so little about my own interaction with my students? Reading Karen's narrative, I can't help but see over and over again the significant role her branch-campus students have played in the choices she made. They are clearly central to her experience. Aren't they to mine as well? In my heart, I know that they are, but in this essay they are strangely invisible.

That makes me uncomfortable. Particularly when I read the last portion of Karen's story where the students, for the only time in her writing, also fade into the background. Is it in the nature of pursuing a career that other considerations about one's location (such as earning tenure and promotion, establishing a relationship with colleagues at both the two-year and four-year campuses of our universities, finding a place within the profession) must take precedence? Karen's anecdotes were about her students; mine were about interactions with colleagues, administrators, and editors. Reading what Karen has written reminds me of the subtext to what I have written—my own students, of whom Karen herself was a most significant one. As I continue to confront the daily issues—and I find them to be daily still—of just how where I am defines who I am, I don't want to lose sight of the students who are also, clearly, confronting that same issue themselves every day. Is this the way it is for all college professors or is this the way it is for two-year college professors? That I truly don't know.

Note

1. Some campuses in the Ohio branch system work differently than mine. Some of my colleagues at other branch campuses are held to precisely the same standards for scholarship that their colleagues at the main campus are. At those branch campuses, despite heavier course loads consisting primarily of lower-division, labor-intensive writing courses, the faculty are expected to publish a single-authored book in their academic specialty. Their home institutions function as if where they are is not in any sense a factor in who they are.

Works Cited

Alford, B., & K. Kroll. 1997. "Scholarship, Tenure, and Composition Studies in the Two-Year College." In *Academic Advancement in Composition Studies: Scholarship, Promotion, and Tenure,* ed. R. Gebhardt & B. Gebhardt, 57–70. Mahwah, NJ: Lawrence Erlbaum.

Aschauer, A. B. 1972. *College Composition at Miami, 1994–95.* Oxford, OH: Miami University.

Bambara, T. 1972. "The Lesson." In *Literature: The Human Experience,* ed. R. Abcarian & M. Klotz, 49–55. 6th edition, 1994. New York: St. Martin's.

Dziech, B., & W. Vilter. 1992. "Editor's Notes." *Prisoners of Elitism: The Community College's Struggle for Stature,* ed. B. Dziech & W. Vilter. San Francisco: Jossey-Bass. New Directions for Community Colleges 78 (2): 1–7.

Greive, D. 1990. *A Handbook for Adjunct/Part-Time Faculty and Teachers of Adults.* Cleveland: Info-Tec, Inc.

Harkin, P., & J. Schilb. 1991. "Introduction." In *Contending with Words: Composition and Rhetoric in a Postmodern Age,* ed. P. Harkin & J. Schilb. 1–10. New York: MLA.

Kort, M. 1994. "Crossing the Great Divide: From the Two-Year College to the University, and Back." *Teaching English in the Two-Year College* 21 (3): 177–82.

Kroll, K. 1990. "Building Communities: Joining the Community of Professional Writing Teachers." *Teaching English in the Two-Year College* 17 (2): 103–07.

———. 1992. "Empowering Faculty as Teacher-Researchers." In *Fostering a Climate for Faculty Scholarship at Community Colleges,* ed. J. Palmer & G. Vaughan,

23–38. Washington, DC: American Association of Community and Junior Colleges.

LaPaglia, N. 1994. Storytellers: *The Image of the Two-Year College in American Fiction and in Women in Journals.* DeKalb, IL: LEPS Press.

McGrath, D., & M. Spear. 1991. *The Academic Crisis of the Community College.* Albany: SUNY P.

Muse, C. 1990. "Celebrating the Community and Junior College." *Teaching English in the Two-Year College* 17 (2): 75–77.

Nist, E., & H. Raines. 1993. "A Search for Community College Voices." In *Writing Ourselves into the Story: Unheard Voices from Composition Studies,* ed. S. Fontaine and S. Hunter, 293–321. Carbondale: Southern Illinois UP.

North, S. 1987. *The Making of Knowledge in Composition.* Portsmouth, NH: Boynton/Cook.

Ratliff, J. 1992. "Scholarship, the Transformation of Knowledge, and Community College Teaching." In *Fostering a Climate for Faculty Scholarship at Community Colleges,* ed. J. Palmer & G. Vaughan, 39–47. Washington, DC: American Association of Community and Junior Colleges.

Shor, I. 1987. *Critical Teaching and Everyday Life.* Chicago: U of Chicago P.

Sommers, J. 1985. "The 'Paradigm Shift' in Composition Instruction: Are Our Students Shifting with Us?" *English in the Two-Year College* 17 (1): 1–5.

Tuell, C. 1993. "Composition Teaching as 'Women's Work': Daughters, Handmaids, Whores, and Mothers." In *Writing Ourselves into the Story: Unheard Voices from Composition Studies,* ed. S. Fontaine and S. Hunter, 123–39. Carbondale: Southern Illinois UP.

Vaughan. G. 1992. "The Community College Unbound." In *Prisoners of Elitism: The Community College's Struggle for Stature,* ed. B. Dziech & W. Vilter. San Franciso, Jossey-Bass. New Directions for Community Colleges 78 (2): 23–34.

———. 1994. "Scholarship and Teaching: Crafting the Art." In *Two-Year College English: Essays for a New Century,* ed. M. Reynolds, 212–21. Urbana, IL: NCTE.

3

The Problem of the Majority Contingent Faculty in the Community Colleges

Helena Worthen

"The best thing about contingent faculty is that you can get rid of them whenever you want."

> —A president of a California community college, spring 1992; a remark made in the presence of contingent faculty

"Little creativity occurs when faculty members are preoccupied with issues of personal security and institutional fairness."

> —Terry O'Banion, *The Renaissance of Innovation*

In studies of community-college issues, one or two pages out of several hundred will be typically spent deploring the overreliance of most colleges on contingent faculty (see Brint & Karabel 1989; Deegan & Tillery 1985; McGrath & Spear 1991; Richardson, Fisk, & Okun 1983). Because contingent faculty are now the substantial majority of community-college faculty (66 percent according to Mahoney & Jimenez 1992), two pages out of several hundred seems, at least to contingent faculty, like a misrepresentation of the situation. Furthermore, most descriptions of the status of faculty in the community colleges are made from the perspectives of administrators, who tend to view their work as managing an organizational structure, or from the perspectives of full-time faculty, who tend to view their work as sustaining a certain norm of academic quality and commitment on behalf of the college as a whole. From both perspectives, contingent faculty appear to be marginal, the exceptions to the norm that provide specific, narrow value. In terms of fiscal logic, they provide flexibility; in terms of curricular planning, they provide the special expertise. However, these descriptions fail to portray what the contingent majority experiences.

In this chapter, I will try to write about the experience of contingent faculty from the point of view of the part-time faculty.

Impossible Choices

A contingent faculty member describes her situation at her college:

> This semester I had a very bad class. There were a lot of people in there who shouldn't have been—relatives, friends who just tagged along. I let them in because if my enrollment had fallen below twenty-five, I would have lost the class. As it was, there were just twenty-five. The result was, I gave out sixteen D's out of twenty-five students. I know this looks bad. I went to a full-timer and asked her what to do. She said, raise all the grades 5 percent. I worked the numbers every way I could and gave them all five extra points. Another full-timer said to just raise all the grades one letter. But the thing is, this was a really bad class. Many of them should have been sent to adult school instead. So I don't want to send them the wrong message. But I'm afraid the dean will look at my grades and say, "You don't belong in the community-college system. You're not in the community-college mode. You don't know your students very well. You don't adjust your teaching to your students." I'm really scared: this could be my job.

This contingent is racked by conflicting responsibilities. To prevent her class from being canceled, she must enroll at least twenty-five students. Although this is too many for the class she is teaching (remedial language arts), she is not in a position to criticize district policy. Minimum class size is set at the district level and is derived from budgetary assumptions. (Specifically, one year's state funding per full-time equivalent (FTE) times twenty-five will support one full-time teacher plus the equal amount of administrative overhead; this means that the difference between full-time and contingent salaries is the "savings" out of which district contingency and discretionary funding comes.[1])

"Not in a position" in this case should be taken literally: There is no secure footing from which this contingent faculty member can speak, no legitimate channel through which her knowledge of the minimum pedagogically sound conditions of her classroom can enter the discussion out of which comes the decision to set class size at twenty-five. There is no feedback loop from the instructor in the classroom to the district management. Although there is faculty representation on the district budget committee, contingents are never on it and information about the classroom work of contingents is not solicited in the decision-making process. So this teacher's options are to accept the students or lose the class. Losing the class means losing the income. Furthermore, she is a forty-year-old single female with no savings, a health problem, and she gets her health insurance through a district group plan (although she pays the premium). So she accepts the class of twenty-five students.

This semester, however, the high minimum class size has meant accepting some students who are unprepared or uncommitted. She worries about this; she knows what the consequences of this may be at exam time. And, sure enough, her fears are realized. At the end of the semester, she knows that if she grades honestly, her grade sheet will be more than half D's. It will look as if she either hasn't taught the students anything or has lost control of the class. When the department grade sheets are compared at the end of the semester, hers will stand out. She is right when she says that her dean will warn her she is not "in the community-college mode." The happy-face tradition of community colleges that calls tutorial centers "success centers" encourages grade sheets that either show a bell curve (indicating a competitive classroom that sorts students[2]) or all A's and B's (the egalitarian outcome). Exceptions to this stand out. Those whom she perceives as judging her include not only her dean, who hires the contingent faculty from one semester to another, but her full-time colleagues, who evaluate her and will sit on any hiring committee to which she will apply if a full-time job opens up in the future. Therefore, faced with an impossible choice, she decides to be proactive and ask their advice. At least for a few moments during the conversation she may hope to display the appropriate amount of exasperation at the conditions that have put her in this bind.

However, their advice to her essentially tells her to set aside her professional integrity. They see themselves as being helpful and supportive by advising her to adapt to coercive circumstances. They do not use the protection of their tenure to address those circumstances themselves. She (again) is not in a position to point this out to them. She is embarrassed on their behalf (embarrassed by their cowardice, as she perceives it), yet she is afraid to say what she thinks of them.

The details of this instructor's experience are an important part of what must be considered when understanding teaching in the community-college system —the "teaching colleges," as they are ironically known. No matter how much this instructor has read, how well she has grasped the arguments of David Bartholomae, Mike Rose, Min-Zhan Lu, Martin Nystrand, Andrea Lunsford, Mina Shaughnessey, or the other contemporary theorists of composition instruction, no theory, no disciplinary knowledge will help her when she faces a class half full of students who shouldn't be there, who are there because the bus doesn't leave until ten-thirty and their ride is enrolled in the class. All the theory in the world won't help her when she is told by someone whose goodwill she depends on to "raise all the grades one letter." In fact, she does read theory. This particular instructor has a Ph.D. She keeps up with the journals in her field and pays her own way to conferences. But how will professional development help her at a moment like this?

What would her knowledge of these impossible choices contribute to a discussion about initiation into the culture of the academy, polyvocalism, dialogic pedagogy, and the appropriation of discursive forms? It is at a moment like this that the concerns of this instructor's disciplinary specialty do not seem contiguous to the realities of her work.

People who are or who know contingents in the community-college system will wonder how I got this story. Stories like this do not float around as general gossip. They are told either in confidence, between people who have reason to trust each other, or else (with bitterness) by former contingents after they have left teaching. Therefore, people might think this is my story because no one would have told it to me. However, it is not my story. In fact, for about seven years I was in a position to hear many stories like that one because between 1988 and 1995 I was part of a general organizing drive to unionize California community-college contingent faculty and to negotiate job-security contract items for contingents in districts where unions were established. Working for the California Federation of Teachers, I edited a newsletter dedicated to this organizing drive. My phone number was listed in the newsletter, and, therefore, I became one of the ears for innumerable stories like this one, stories that could not be told to anyone local whom the troubled contingent knew because, without job security, to name a problem was to be a problem.

Here is another story. This is not a language-arts instructor. It is a carpentry instructor. Language arts and carpentry tend to inhabit different hemispheres of the educational globe, but note the parallels in the issues: class-size determination made at a distance, compromises made by the teacher, devaluation of educational experience, and the collusion of the tenured full-timer who wants to be helpful but does not attempt to use his or her protected status to address the problem at its root. This story also explicitly mentions the absence of a communication channel from the instructor to the administration, and the way in which the instructor's working conditions block the flow of information from the instructor to the decision-making part of the system. I offer this story to make the point that the politics of teaching anything as a contingent overwhelm the politics of a specific discipline. This is precisely because the conditions of contingent teaching silence debate about disciplinary concerns: to disagree fundamentally about how to do your job with someone who has power over your job is to risk losing your job. The only situations in which the power relations between contingent faculty and the rest of the college personnel do not matter with regard to disciplinary issues are those in which all debate has been *a priori* extinguished and there is nothing left to disagree about. It is a situation that can be achieved, of course (and is often attempted), by routinizing all aspects of teaching.

The carpentry instructor told me this story:

This semester they just jammed me, jammed me for ADA (average daily attendance). I have thirty-five students in every class, no more than two absences on any day, and they're sticking with me, not dropping. But I can only handle twenty-five in the shop. Now I haven't had an accident in there the whole time

I've been working here, but I don't have eyes in the back of my head, and this semester, I got really worried. The students have insurance and worker's comp, but still, you don't want an accident. I went to a full-timer who teaches wood technology and asked him what I should do and he just said, "Hang in there." What I did was, I didn't let the students get their hands on power tools at all until halfway through the semester. Now if I had had job security, I would have said to the administration, "No, it's not safe, I won't take any more than twenty-five, I won't sign the add cards." And they would have just had to live with it.

This instructor has safety concerns: power tools can cut off a finger or a hand. An unsupervised student could start a fire by plugging extension cords into the wrong socket. Applying varnish in an unventilated corner could make a student pass out. Here, learning to use equipment is analogous to learning to write; the problem of instrumentality, of learning to make a tool serve one's purpose, is the same. In both cases, the instructor's hope of teaching students to use something is defeated.

The two disciplines—carpentry and composition—may seem unalike, but when they are both taught by contingents their similarities are more salient than their differences.

The Snapshot Survey

"If I had some job security . . . " became words familiar to us as our team of organizers expanded to include people at more colleges, and more and more stories like this came to our ears, stories that could only be entrusted to those of us who had earned credibility by publicly working to change the conditions that were causing the conflicts.

After four or five years of working on this effort, I began to feel inhabited by these voices. I got so I jumped when the phone rang at dinner and a voice said, "I don't think you know me, but I got your name from the union. . . ." Then I would hear a fifty-five-year-old teacher of French who was being replaced by another, younger teacher who "had better energy." I would hear a Chinese teacher of physics, who was caught explaining a concept (after class, to his mostly Chinese students) in Chinese, by a non-Chinese administrator and was being descheduled (a euphemism) because he is "racist." I would hear a young Spanish teacher who was nominated by her students as Teacher of the Year and was now being told by her dean that she had developed "a bad attitude." And there was the young man who became active in his union (at a college where contingent faculty could buy into the health plan) and tried to organize contingents; he suddenly had no assignment. I couldn't help him; the union could not be mobilized to prove retaliation. We heard a year later that he had died of AIDS, without health insurance.

In all these stories, contingent teachers were asked or told to do something (or not to do something) that discredited or suppressed their own experience and knowledge—of their students, of their own work lives, of their disciplines. Their seniority, their bilingualism, their pride, their bravery; they each paid dearly for these.

These were difficult years for me. There were times when I could not bring myself to have a civil conversation with an administrator whom I knew from another source to have exploited the vulnerability of a contingent, or with a full-time faculty member who had failed to use his or her protected status to lessen that vulnerability.

I began to want to make these stories public. They had been told us in confidence, as part of a request for help (I have changed some details to disguise the situations I've described), so they could not be used for newsletter articles or for a study, for example, to create a cumulative, aggregate portrait. Therefore, eventually our organizing team decided to ask for, rather than just wait for, such stories. We sent out two hundred copies of a one-page survey asking people to write a few sentences, or more if they wished, about the relationship between their ability to do their jobs well and their job security. Anonymous responses were fine, but we warned people that we would use the stories they told us publicly. We asked both full- and part-time faculty and we asked at campuses where there was no job security for contingents as well as at campuses where there was a degree of job security (some kind of due process, usually). The survey was supposed to be a snapshot of how people felt at that moment in time.

We got back forty responses. One person, afraid to be identified, phoned me after mailing in his response and asked me to pull it from the stack. Another wrote, in response to our question about experiences illustrating the connection between job security and quality of work, "Not on paper, not in my handwriting!" These responses created a picture of an academic culture overcast with fear, and often confused.

Some responses seemed to be just about the banality of evil:

> I was bumped the current semester by a full-timer who had an underenrolled course. He chose my course because it was scheduled for a Tuesday and Thursday. This instructor had been getting his Fridays free for the last six years.

> One semester, my teaching schedule was changed at the last minute. I said I couldn't work that schedule and expressed anger over the situation. I was not called to teach the next semester, presumably because I didn't quietly go along with things.

> I won an election against a full-timer for a prestigious post in the honors program. He tried to have me fired; threatened me; tried to invalidate the elections; and finally cursed me, shoved me, and hit me. Thankfully, the union reprimanded him, and the administration followed suit.

I knew, from previous conversations with many people like those who answered our survey, that they loved their students and their disciplines and had a vision of good teaching. Yet when asked about their relationship to the colleges where they worked, their enthusiasm failed and they became evasive and timid. Some responses revealed contingents taking proactive measures to create a publicly safe or pleasing persona:

> I suspect that "charm" may be valued over academic accomplishments, ability to teach.

> Sometimes your teaching can be changed to conform to the powers that be.

> Anyone who says they teach exactly the same way as they would if they had full tenure is either a fool or not teaching much worth learning.

> As a contingent who wants a full-time job, I am perpetually auditioning.

> Even though I take what I believe to be the correct stance (academic, pedagogic, or political), there is always the worry that the "wrong" person will hear and disapprove. I definitely have the impression from other [contingents] that they feel the same way. One feels constantly endangered.

> As a contingent, I was threatened more than once with the possibility of losing my classes if I didn't fall into line with department policies. These included content as well as scheduling. I had to put up with a lot of unprofessional behavior.

> There is subtle pressure to post grades that look like the rest of the department (not too many D's or A's, depending on the current fad).

Others displayed a kind of quiet defiance:

> My pride will not allow me to slack even though I have no contract.

> I do a serious job in spite of being an adjunct teacher.

> I don't allow insecurity to affect me. More security, more risks one might take in terms of pedagogy, content. However, those without security might still take risks.

We asked if there were substantive issues to disagree about. Examples came from all different disciplines:

> Using material represented by the white male canon leads to different discussion than a more multicultural selection. If a dean prefers to teach one set of values, lifestyles, goals over another, your job may be jeopardized if you fall into the latter category.

> Philosophy can by nature be controversial.

> I personally know people who have been let go for their choice of texts.

> History is inherently political all the time.

> The anti-immigrant movement bears directly on our dealings with ESL [English as a Second Language] speakers in composition class.

> High standards for university transfer classes are being sacrificed to keep large classes. If an instructor holds high standards (a contingent instructor, that is), she is accused of "not being nice to students."

Some instructors dealt with the politics of their discipline by simply skirting anything controversial. We heard from a psychologist who stuck to what he considered "objective" and a chemist who avoided talking about environmental issues:

> There is certainly enough to talk about that is objective in psychology, without getting into very many political issues. I am not all that much wishing to mix politics with my discipline.

> Not much in chemistry. Except in environmental policy. . . . But one must feel secure to discuss one's true feelings.

Others, especially ESL and basic-skills instructors, faced the issue directly:

> Teaching ESL is definitely political . . . I give my students examples of people struggling and improving their lives. I'm not just giving them skills to they can go out and earn more money and better themselves individually. It's collective betterment. Their problems are not individual, their problems are part of a group.

> How can anyone teach basic skills to inner-city young people without asking why economically disadvantaged people are so often educationally disadvantaged as well?

> My students are not in remedial classes because they are genetically inferior; they are there because of the world they live in, and I have to help them learn to either change it or else escape from it.

Look closely at the last clause of that statement: "learn to either change [the world] or else escape from it." It implies a certain curriculum, for which there is plenty of support in the adult-education literature (see Friere 1985; Newman 1994; Rose 1989). This may seem like a laudable, unexceptional goal for a remedial language-arts teacher, but what would become of her if she persisted in this goal after a dean decided that remedial classes should teach to a skills-focused exit test?

The logical next step for those who do their best despite not having job security is to feel contempt for faculty who have the protection of tenure but seem to be doing nothing with it. These people are an advance guard in the mounting effort to eliminate tenure:

> Job security makes some teachers fat, dumb, and happy.

> I personally feel that job security does not always nurture academic excellence: in fact, it creates inefficiency.

> Tenure permits long-term mediocrity.

> Incompetent faculty stay as long as the best of us.

Quite a few saw a connection between the job status of individual faculty and the life of the college as a whole.

> More workshops and more communication between and for faculty would occur if there were more job security.

Long-range planning on curriculum, designing and revamping programs, can only come from someone who has a full-time position. But many full-time faculty mentioned quitting teaching:

> My advice to new contingent instructors in the community-college system is to find other work. I blew it! If I had my life to do over again, I would go to work for United Airlines. I would not have invested the time, effort, and emotional capital trying to be a good teacher.

Incidentally, at about the time that we gathered these responses, I took a look at the quit rates of contingents in my own district and found that 50 percent of all contingents were gone within two years of being hired. Another organizer at another district did the same study and found the same quit rate.

These were the disturbing responses that our organizing team got when we asked contingents to summarize their experience for public consumption. With a few exceptions, they told us: I am angry, but I keep a smile on my face for my administrative manager; I try to forget about lack of job security; my discipline has deeply rooted debates, but I play it safe and don't refer to them; I don't think teachers with tenure deserve it, and I wouldn't advise anyone to go into teaching. The tone is low key and controlled (unlike the stories I would hear in phone calls, when the speaker was likely to be weeping). The overall impression these stories give me is of people who have adapted to denying to themselves a major portion of the knowledge created by their own work lives.

Unfortunately, these responses deal with instructor-administrator and instructor-student relationships only. A type of relationship we did not ask people to comment on is that between instructors, among colleagues. How much collegiality is possible when instructors are in competition with each other for the scarce resource of the approval of a manager, which leads to getting rehired? How much does the need to continually please those who have the power to hire distort the part-timers' contribution to any college infrastructure work he or she may participate in?

Conversations Minus One Voice

My own exposure to the inside stories of contingent faculty made me highly sensitive to discussions of community-college policy in which the voices of part-timers is absent. The public conversation about contingents takes place overwhelmingly among full-time faculty or among administrators, over the heads, as it were, of contingents, which means that space in the discourse gets taken up by people who do not know the whole story. As a result, we get articles like the full-page personal essay in the *Chronicle of Higher Education,* written by Eugene Arden, a vice-chancellor emeritus at the University of Michigan. Arden tells how, each semester, he tried to create an opportunity for "a collegial encounter" among contingents (a three-hour weekend breakfast or lunch in the faculty dining room). He reports that at one such encounter there was a discussion of the value of "including some classroom discussion rather than lecturing for the full period." At other sessions he brought in an expert on testing or showed a video about ethnic and gender issues. Now, these contingents were not novice teachers; in fact, Arden even mentions that "a sizeable number are travelers, who manage to piece together a low-paying full-time schedule by teaching four or five courses per semester on two or even three campuses." Yet Arden makes no mention of asking them to tell him (or each other) about their work; he assumes that they are the empty pails that he must fill. How can he imagine that they need to be told to include opportunities for discussion during a lecture? The only time we hear their voices is when they are expressing gratitude: "I was told more than once: 'This is the first time the institution has paid any attention to us.' Another adjunct asked, 'Does all of this activity mean that what we do in the classroom really matters to you?'" Arden does not tell what the next turn in that dialogue was. Maybe there was none. But if Arden had replied, "Yes, what you do in the classroom really matters," then the adjunct might have said, "Well, then, if that is the case, why don't you be quiet for a moment and listen to us tell you about it?"

Another example, an article in *Crosstalk* (January 1995, 5), a policy newsletter published by the California Higher Education Policy Center in San Jose, describes the shift of remedial English composition courses from the University of California at Davis to Sacramento City Community College, a controversial move occurring as part of a general narrowing of access to the UC system under fiscal stress. The choice to narrow access rather than broaden support for public higher education in California has been made in the context of noisy legislative debate, high-profile partisan politics, and lots of news coverage; the removal of basic English to the community colleges is a highly visible link in that process. Not incidentally (because cost-savings are the driving concern), all of the teachers of the thirty-one sections of the relocated class are contingents. Not one of them is quoted, which makes it possible for readers to get a description of the program and a judgment on the success of the program without ever hearing testimony from someone actually teaching in the program who might be able to comment on the significance of the increase in class size from fifteen to eighteen students per class (the norm at UC) to thirty per class, or how they manage to teach a composition class without paid office hours in which to hold student conferences. William Twombly, the reporter, interviewed everyone else, apparently: the coordinator of the program at The University of California at Davis, the coordinator at Sacramento City, an instructor at Davis who used to teach the course when it was run through Davis, the retired chemistry professor from Davis who set up the program, the president of Sacramento City, and a coordinator of a similar program at University of California at San Diego. There is no evidence that he interviewed someone who was teaching the course. The article does tell us that the teachers are paid about $40 an hour—$50 if they have a Ph.D. Twombly says that the program will be imitated "because the taxpayers are going to demand it." In what other field or business would such a judgment be made without even inquiring after the opinion of the people who know the most about how the program is working?

My point is not that *Crosstalk* makes a unique error, but that the absence of the perspective of the teacher from reports of teaching is so prevalent that it passes unnoted. The employment of faculty in part-time positions is treated as a policy matter, not a pedagogical matter. The silence of the majority of faculty in discussions of policy is a nonissue.

The Working Conditions of
the Typical Community-College Instructor

Today the modal community-college faculty person is contingent. This makes community colleges a qualitatively different place than when the part-timers were the visiting experts or emergency temporary help.

Contingent faculty were not always the modal faculty. On August 17, 1995, in a radio broadcast about the community-college system on the NPR show *Talk of the Nation,* Arthur Cohen of the ERIC Clearinghouse said that there had been no significant change in the proportion of part-time faculty over the last thirty years. He could hardly have been more wrong. According to the Spring 1990 ERIC Information Bulletin, "Between 1973 and 1984, the number of full-time faculty increased by 22 percent, whereas the number of part-time faculty grew by 168 percent."

In 1980, Edmund Gleazer, past president of the American Association of Community Colleges (AACC), articulated the traditional academic rationale for hiring contingents to bring in "special expertise." Gleazer explained:

> A large number of faculty are active in the practice of their trade and profession as well as in their teaching. Sometimes referred to as "professor-practitioners" or adjunct professors, they work as real-estate insurance brokers, lawyers, engineers, craftsmen, and doctors and provide further means for linking up with other parts of the community's learning system. (11)

These contingents could make the college a multiplier of community culture and skills. Gleazer did not envision a faculty that was predominantly part-time. His contingent faculty were part-time because they had other full-time jobs outside teaching; that is what gave them "special expertise." Nor did he foresee that they would be used to solve budget problems or reduce the influence of tenured faculty.

Time passed. The boom years of physical expansion of colleges were over. Now the problem was to fill the buildings with students, maximize enrollment, without spending too much money, and the obvious answer was to hire contingent faculty. In 1989, the Conference on College Composition and Communication produced what is known as the Wyoming Resolution (Robertson, Crowley, & Lentricchia 1987), against the overuse of contingents. The National Education Association generated a "Report and Recommendations on Part-Time, Temporary and Non-Tenure Track Faculty Appointments." The Modern Language Association also produced a position statement. In 1992, the Association of Departments of English declared that "the conditions under which most adjunct teachers are employed define them as nonprofessionals." The American Federation of Teachers, which had produced one position statement in 1979, produced another. Faculty organizations (unions, associations, and disciplinary organizations) were across-the-board critical of the overuse of part-time faculty.

However, by this time the budgetary appeal of a low-cost faculty was enhanced by the management appeal of a "flexible" faculty. Linda Pratt in *Report on the Status of Non-Tenure Track Faculty* (1992) summarized 1991 data from National Center for Education Statistics on contingents in higher education. They noted that while the use of contingent faculty might have originated as a way to save money, it had evolved into a mechanism for creating budgetary discretion. The power to choose how to spend the saved money had become a motive for saving money in the first place:

> . . . since 1970 part-time appointments as a proportion of all faculty appointments have risen from 21.9 percent to 33.9 percent in 1987 . . . closer examination of the data indicates that most of the relative growth of part-time faculty occurred during the period from 1972 to 1977, a period often characterized as one of sharply reduced financial strength for both private and public institutions, and increased institutional interest in alternatives to the tenure system. If those events are important causes of the growth of part-time faculty, then the fact that the supposedly temporary situation did not improve after the economic recovery suggests a growing administrative desire for budgetary discretion. (43)

The collision of "budgetary discretion" with academic quality was becoming a central concern. In 1993, Judith Gappa and David Leslie published *The Invisible Faculty: Improving the Status of Part-Timers in Higher Education.* They argued for a respectful treatment of contingents as employees and professionals, including better professional development programs, careful evaluations, and job stability:

> We cannot think of a better investment for a college or university than its faculty. We think that relatively small investments in part-time faculty now will

pay off over the next decade, when the faculty workforce will experience tur-
bulent times. (283)

But the threefold logic for relying on contingents continues to grind inexorably
forward: Part-timers bring expertise, save money, and increase management discretion, an unbeatable combination. The result is more part-timers.

In October 1994, the National Center for Education Statistics (NCES 1995)
reported that there were 253,711 faculty and instructional staff as of fall 1992,
of which 53.4 percent or 135 out of 518 were contingent (1–2). The NCES count,
however, did not include instructors teaching in noncredit programs (where large
numbers of contingents teach remedial-skills classes, ESL, and composition)
or instructors in contract education programs. In addition, the NCES survey
counted persons with faculty status whose assignments did not include instruction (such as some deans, researchers, administrators) and persons on sabbati-
cal, the exclusion of whom would decrease the numbers of full-time faculty and
thereby increase the percentage of faculty recorded as part-time (19). Furthermore, both the NCES and the AACC surveys were based on self-reports, leaving
it to the individual institutions to define who is contingent and who is not. Both
surveys probably underestimated the numbers of contingents.

As Perry Robinson (1994) points out, critiquing the previous (1988) NCES
survey, "There is no national standard definition of a regular part-time faculty
member," which gives institutions considerable reporting leeway (9). He lists
the four states with the highest percentages of contingent community college
faculty: Vermont (100 percent); Illinois (73.6 percent); Pennsylvania (73.3 percent), and Ohio (72.7 percent). California alone had 26,727 contingents and
16,012 full-timers in the fall of 1993 (California Postsecondary Education Commission 1994, 17). That means that 62.5 percent of faculty in the California
community colleges were contingents in 1993. The California count is regarded
as reasonably accurate because, since the major California Community College
Reform Bill AB 1725, which attempted to penalize districts that hired contingents to teach over 25 percent of credit classes, it is watched closely by several
competing constituencies.

The increase in low-cost, flexible contingents mirrors the increase in contingent labor throughout the economy. Robinson places part-time teaching in the
context of other part-time work:

> Labor Department statistics reveal that some occupations have an even higher
> rate of part-time employment than higher education: food counter, foun-
> tain, and related workers, 70.9 percent; library assistants and bookmobile driv-
> ers, 63 percent; ushers and lobby attendants, 72.8 percent; child-care work-
> ers, 61.6 percent; and guards, 86.5 percent. (1994, 4)

However, he points out that:

> . . . among "professional specialty occupations" only the two categories
> of dancers/choreographers and musicians have a higher incidence of part-

time employment than higher education faculty. And if only two-year college faculty were considered, higher education would have the highest percentage. (4, 5)

Because this book is about the politics of writing instruction, it is important to note that contingents are concentrated in programs that have seen enrollment increases in the last twenty years, such as remedial programs, ESL programs, and composition, all of which may be organized under Humanities, Language Arts, or English departments and any of which may offer the college's writing courses. Part-time faculty members float among these departments, working wherever they can get a course. Kroll (1994) surveyed public and private community colleges in the nineteen-state Council of North Central Two-Year Colleges and estimated that the proportion per institution of instructors of English who are part-time faculty is around 62 percent.

Contingents, then, have become the modal faculty members. When we say that they teach under conditions in which they are likely to be fearful of losing their jobs, cannot participate fully or honestly in the institutional discourse, and lack encouragement or material support for professional development, we should remember that we're talking about the working conditions of the typical community-college instructor. Tenure is not the norm; tenure is the exception and insecurity is the norm. Writing in the *Golden Gate University Law Review,* Jeffrey Kerwin said, "The complete exposure of part-time teachers to arbitrary or repressive action has a chilling effect on their exercise of freedom of speech" (1980, 81). Because contingents are the modal community-college faculty, that sentence ought to read, "The complete exposure of *community-college* teachers to arbitrary or repressive action has a chilling effect on their exercise of freedom of speech." When this happens, all the activities that evolve in the infrastructure of an academic institution—the discussion, the reflection upon work, the collaboration, the development of new programs—become severed from their roots in the classroom, where the real knowledge of the institution accumulates.

Education policy does not yet reflect this fact. Understanding this—that the actual faculty working in the community colleges is contingent faculty working under unsatisfactory conditions—and integrating it into our assessments of the mission of higher education, into our state and local oversight and regulatory policies, and into our education school-training curriculum would require a major rethinking of the meaning of work in academia.

The NCRVE Study of Teaching in the Community Colleges

By the early 1990s I had gone back to graduate school at Berkeley, in part because I had encountered some questions about teaching and learning that I could not answer without drawing on resources that lay well beyond the walls of my classroom. I had the good luck to get a graduate research assistantship working for Dr. W. Norton Grubb on an empirical study, funded by the National Center for Research in Vocational Education, of teaching in the community colleges. The purpose of the study was to develop an aggregate empirically based portrait of what goes on in community-college classrooms. This information is typically reported in case-study form or in terms of outcomes (number of students enrolled, retained, passed, placed, etc.). We wanted to fill the gap in the literature by actually going to see what was happening. We eventually visited thirty-two community colleges and observed 250 classrooms, interviewing instructors and administrators. This project enabled me to visit community colleges outside of California as well as to interview administrators.

Approaching community colleges through the administration, as a researcher rather than through the union as an organizer, was, as I had expected, a different experience. Upon arriving at a college I would typically be given a list of instructors to observe. My letter of introduction had asked to be allowed to observe instructors in a range of disciplines — occupational and technical, liberal arts, contingent and full-time. Usually the list would have no contingents on it. I would ask my administrator contact if it would be possible to observe a contingent faculty member. Often, it simply wasn't possible; they didn't have complete lists and didn't know how to get in touch with the contingent.

At one college in Iowa I was assured that there were no contingents. Later that day, after interviewing a full-time statistics instructor, I asked him how the college had managed to refrain from relying on contingents. "What?" he said. "Come look in the mailroom and I'll show you a whole wall of their boxes."

At another college the only person I met who could talk about contingents was the union vice-president, who had just been handed a proposal for instructor evaluations that did not include an evaluation procedure for contingents. She was angry: "They are the first contact the public has with us, and I want to know if someone's just standing out at the end of a road handing out grades," she said.

We found only one community college, Indian Hills, that did not use any part-time faculty. It expressly had a policy against "going the part-timer route." However, it was located in a rural area of Iowa, well off the freeway flyer route, and had no adjacent colleges that could have generated a critical mass of jobs for contingents. Most of the faculty at this college actually used the metaphor "one happy family" when I asked them how policy and governance decisions were made.

By comparison, other colleges used as many contingents as they could hire. Union roles varied enormously; in several states, the faculty union excluded contingents; in another, the union had negotiated contractual job security for contingent faculty and priority for full-time jobs.

Overall, my impression from visiting community colleges outside California was that, with the exception of the colleges where the union had taken up part-time issues actively, contingents were, as Gappa and Leslie (1993) noted, truly "the invisible faculty."

Looking at the Future

Two trends seem to extend into the future of community colleges: the increased use of contingents and adding industry-specific training by region. Perhaps, by noting the ways in which these trends are consistent with each other, it is possible to envision the future of community colleges.

One trend is the seemingly irresistible urge to increase the use of part-time faculty at the community college. There seems to be no brake on it except state-level legislation and unionization, which is neither easy nor a sure thing. The second trend is based on our research during the NCRVE study, which focused on occupational/technical programs. In addition to the traditional community-college missions of occupational/technical, remedial and liberal-arts, and transfer education, a fourth mission is thriving: industry-specific training for regional economic-development purposes. While some colleges had not entered this path at all, others were running a booming operation involving partnerships with industry. In these programs, the community college provides for the industry whatever kind of training the industry wants its workers to have—generic training like computer instruction, total quality management, or statistical process control, or specific training on machines, vehicles, tools, or software that only one manufacturer uses. There is no need to hire full-time faculty for these programs or to involve full-time faculty already at the college to approve or create the curriculum. Running these programs was treated as an entrepreneurial challenge: making the contact, signing the contracts, assigning the room, hiring the instructor, creating (or buying) the curriculum, and collecting the fees. In places where these programs had been set up, they were generating sufficient income for the college that they were seen as an irresistible trend.

These trends, increasing use of contingents and increasing involvement with industry-specific training programs, are not incompatible with each other; on the contrary, they are consistent with and may even amplify each other. They seem, however, to be incompatible with the traditional missions of the community college as open-access, low-cost, second-chance institutions. The result of the combination of these two trends might be to create a segment of higher education that is dedicated to the short-term needs of local industry and is run in an entrepreneurial manner by program planners using contingent instructors as they would independent contractors.

The Politics of Writing Instruction from
the Point of View of Contingent Faculty

I was asked to write about the politics of writing instruction as experienced by contingents; instead, I've written about the politics of instruction in general when it is carried on by contingents. My point is that for contingents, no matter what one is teaching—writing, history, ESL, philosophy, or carpentry—the politics of the workplace overwhelm the politics of the discipline. One of our respondents said, parodying *A Streetcar Named Desire,* "I have always been dependent upon the politics of strangers."

The politics of the world our students come from embraces both the college and the classroom. The job of the community colleges (unless they become primarily instruments of economic development) is to provide educational opportunity for people who want it, but, for either academic or financial reasons, are unable to attend other institutions of higher education. The demographics of the students who are drawn to community colleges reflect this in their numbers: Of all minorities enrolled in higher education as of 1992, 47 percent were in community colleges. Fifty-eight percent of the students enrolled in fall 1992 were women; the typical woman had at least one child and was working part-time. Twenty-seven percent were minority. Eight percent were disabled; more than half of all disabled students in college were in community colleges. (Phillippe 1995, 20–21). The politics of writing instruction is embedded in the politics of the community college as workplace, which is in turn embedded in the politics of being disadvantaged—minority, female, a single parent, a part-time worker, low-income, or disabled—in the United States. The politics of the world students live in penetrates to the center of this dense arrangement where it hardly matters whether one is a composition instructor or a carpentry instructor. This statement was made by a contingent carpentry instructor: "We begin with the wood, and maybe it's redwood, and we go from there to the redwood tree, and the forest, and pretty soon it's the spotted owl." The story the instructor is telling pushes back out through the dense concatenation of contexts; if he or she is very skilled, or exceptionally lucky, this instructor may be able to keep the story moving and carry the students back past all the hazards they overcame to get to the classroom, back to a world that he encourages them to weave together in a coherent master narrative.

But doing that, pushing the boundaries, entails risks, and the instructor may decide: "I say to myself, no, wait, I'm just supposed to be teaching them carpentry." And the carpenter's last line might easily have been said by a contingent composition instructor: "Sometimes I would like to give them the whole world, but I hold myself back."

Notes

1. This calculation describes the California situation, where most of the college funding comes from the state at the rate of about $3,700 per FTE per year. In other states, where the state may supply as little as 40 percent of college funding and where college districts set their tuition cost locally, a different formula holds, but the incentive to hire contingent faculty remains the same: tenured or continuing-contract faculty are a fixed cost, whereas contingent faculty are cheap and flexible.

2. In fact, contingent faculty members are more likely than full-time faculty to use a bell curve in grading students, according to the June 1995 issue of the *National Edu-*

cation Association Higher Education Research Center Update, a report generated from the data of the 1993 National Study of Postsecondary Faculty by the National Center for Education Statistics. Comparing part-time and full-time faculty in terms of the way each group evaluates students' work (the possible categories were student presentations, student evaluations, multiple-choice tests, essay tests, short-answer tests, term or research papers, multiple drafts of written work, grading on a curve, and competency-based grading), the report finds that part-time teachers tend to be more conservative than full-timers in their evaluation techniques (NEA 1995, 3). My interpretation is that contingents evaluate conservatively because they teach defensively.

Works Cited

American Federation of Teachers. April 7, 1979. *Statement on Part-Time Faculty Employment.* American Federation of Teachers Advisory Commission on Higher Education. Washington D.C.: AFT.

Arden, E. July 21, 1995. *Ending the Loneliness and Isolation of Adjunct Professors.* Point of View column in *The Chronicle of Higher Education,* A44.

Brint, S., & J. Karabel. 1989. *The Diverted Dream: Community Colleges and the Promise of Educational Opportunity in America, 1900–85.* New York: Oxford Press.

California Postsecondary Education Commission. August 1994. *Faculty Salaries in California's Community Colleges, 1993–94.* Commission Report 94–13. Sacramento: CPEC.

Deegan, W. L., & D. Tillery. 1985. *Renewing the American Community College.* San Francisco: Jossey-Bass.

ERIC Clearinghouse for Junior Colleges. Spring 1990. *Information Bulletin.* University of California, Los Angeles.

Friere, P. 1985. *The Politics of Education: Culture, Power and Liberation.* South Hadley: Bergin & Gavney.

Gappa, J. M., & D. W. Leslie. 1993. *The Invisible Faculty: Improving the Status of Part-Timers in Higher Education.* San Francisco, Calif.: Jossey-Bass.

Gleazer, E. J., Jr. 1980. *The Community College: Values, Vision, and Vitality.* Washington, D.C.: AACJC.

Kerwin, J. 1980. "The Part-Time Teacher and Tenure in California." *Golden Gate University Law Review,* 10(2): 765–803.

Kroll, K. 1994. "A Profile and Perspective of Part-Time Two-Year College English Faculty." *Teaching English in the Two-Year College.* (December): 277–87.

Mahoney, J., & E. Jimenez, eds. 1992. *Community, Technical and Junior Colleges Statistical Yearbook.* Washington, D.C.: American Association of Community Colleges.

McGrath, D., & M. Spear. 1991. *The Academic Crisis of the Community Colleges.* Albany: SUNY P.

Modern Language Association. 1982. "MLA Statement on the Use of Part-Time Faculty." *Profession 82.* MLA, 52.

National Center for Education Statistics. October 1994. *Faculty and Instructional Staff: Who Are They and What Do They Do?* Survey Report: 1993 National Study of Postsecondary Faculty. U.S. Department of Education, Office of Educational Research and Improvement. NCES 94–346.

National Center for Education Statistics. 1995. *Fall Staff in Postsecondary Institutions, 1991.* U.S. Department of Education, Office of Educational Research and Improvement. NCES (February): 95–317.

National Education Association. June 1995. *NEA Higher Education Research Center Update.* 1(1). Washington, D.C.: NEA.

Newman, M. 1994. *Defining the Enemy: Adult Education in Social Action.* Paddington, New South Wales: Stewart Victor Publishing.

Phillippe, K. A., editor. 1995. *National Profile of Community Colleges: Trends and Statistics, 1995–1996.* Washington, D.C.: Community College.

Pratt, L. R., et al. November-December 1992. Committee G. on Part-Time and Non-Tenure Track Appointments. "Report on the Status of Non-Tenure Track Faculty." *Academe: The Bulletin of the American Association of University Professors:* 39–48.

President's Commission on Higher Education. 1947. *Higher Education for American Democracy, a Report of the President's Commission on Higher Education.* Washington, D.C.: U.S. Government Printing Office.

O'Banion, T. 1981. "The Renaissance of Innovation." In *Innovation in the Community Colleges,* ed. T. O'Banion. New York: ACE/McMillan.

Richardson, R. C., E. C. Fisk, & M. A. Okun. 1983. *Literacy in the Open Access College.* San Francisco: Jossey-Bass.

Robertson, L. R., S. Crowley, & F. Lentricchia. March 1987. "Opinion: The Wyoming Conference Resolution Opposing Unfair Salaries and Working Conditions for Post-Secondary Teachers of Writing." *College English* 49(3): 274–80.

Robinson, P. June 1994. *Part-Time Faculty Issues.* Washington D.C.: American Federation of Teachers.

Rose, M. 1989. *Lives on the Boundary.* New York: Free Press.

Shor, I. 1986. *Culture Wars: School and Society in the Conservative Revolution.* New York: Routledge.

Twombly, W. January 1995. "English 57: Cooperative Venture Unites UC and Community Colleges." *Crosstalk: A Quarterly Publication of the California Higher Education Policy Center.* 3(1): 5.

4

Basic Writing Textbooks and Corporate Publishing Logic

Can Diversity Work in a Bottom-Line Economy?

Dan Fraizer

Textbooks have been used to construct school curricula at least as far back as sixteenth- and seventeenth-century Europe where mechanically reproduced texts led to reduced reliance on oral instruction and memory. It wasn't until the mid nineteenth century, however, that school *districts* began to build their curricula around textbooks in a systematic way. Delivery of a standardized curriculum began to develop as increasing numbers of elementary schools staffed by semitrained teachers used textbooks to impose structure and "narrow the range of achievement" (Westbury 1990, 5–6).

By the early 1890s, a consolidated publishing industry had capitalized on improved printing techniques and the newly built railroad by selling not just individual books but entire curriculum packages, to dominate an unregulated market (Westbury 1990, 8). Textbook-approval committees were established in twentieth-century public schools, and a pattern of publishers proposing the curriculum and committees disposing of unwanted elements of that curriculum began. Many two-year college teachers and administrators trace their educational roots to K–12 educational systems, so the history of control and structure in U.S. systems provides one context for beginning to better understand the role textbooks play in the two-year or community-college curriculum. The economic markets created as composition became a discipline in its own right provides a second important context. Awareness of both contexts is necessary to a critical understanding of the use of textbooks in basic writing classes today.

The second half of the nineteenth century saw the recorded college lectures of rhetoricians like William Campbell, Hugh Blair, and Joseph Priestly being rewritten by publishers as texts to these men's considerable advantage. Robert Connors has noted that Blair's *Lectures* saw at least sixty-six full-length editions in the United States before 1874 (1986, 180). Not only was the technology to produce these books available, but the explosion of new small colleges and universities meant many inexperienced and untrained teachers were being hired to teach the new students. These teachers chose drill-and-skill texts to quickly and easily implement a classroom curriculum. Connors argues that these new and often overcrowded classrooms influenced the kind of writing done by students. Under these institutional and structural conditions, student writing tended to be "not the sort of writing the teacher needed to look at" (184), which eventually helped to transform a more philosophically inclined rhetoric class into a more highly structured composition class, to the detriment of rhetorical theory, some have argued (Crowley 1990; Welch 1990). By the beginning of the twentieth century, both community colleges as well as elementary and secondary schools were reproducing a cookie-cutter approach to composition using books students could actually write in and use up.

Understanding the origins of the modern composition textbook in the United States is also important to the discussion that follows concerning basic writing textbooks and the publishing industry. Textbooks meant to be used in remedial, compensatory, developmental, or basic writing classes have become problematic for a variety of reasons. One reason has been a less-than-thorough understanding on the part of publishers, editors, and teachers of basic writing students and their needs, as well as, until recently, the absence of an institutionalized structure to meet those needs. While the concept of remediation has been around a long time,[1] there remains no broad agreement about what it is or what it should be. Lack of consensus about remediation has not slowed the development and expansion of programs and departments meant to do "remedial" work, however, especially in two-year schools[2], where open enrollments continued to rise throughout the 1980s. By 1990, 47 percent of developmental reading programs were located at two-year colleges, with the remainder divided between universities and four-year colleges (Bullock, Madden, and Mallery 1990, 34–38).

What is most clear is that wherever it is taught, remedial education[3] is highly politicized because it involves work with those outside of a traditionally accepted population of college students. Remedial education requires teachers to work with students who are less prepared for the demands of traditional college classes. These students are, not coincidentally, also people who typically do not have access to the same resources or conversations as do students attending more prestigious academic institutions. While the development of widespread public education in this country since the nineteenth century has been equated with increased opportunities for the less privileged in general, other factors have limited these opportunities. For example, as curricula began to be controlled by centralized authoritative groups, especially publishers, blame for being "inadequately educated" was conveniently directed toward students who either didn't "work hard enough" or didn't "have what it takes." Publishers often escape blame for student failure, even today when teachers are often convenient scapegoats.

The comparatively recent work of linguists and literacy theorists whose research examines the social and political nature of language and literacy use and construction,[4] has helped all educators to better understand the existence and legitimacy of multiple linguistic communities and the politicized assumptions and conflicts inherent in any discussion of a naturally "superior" dialect or use of language (including writing). It has become less acceptable to reduce remediation to a matter of "working harder" than others to master a dialect of prestige meant to remedy an assumed and usually unspoken linguistic deficiency.

Still, these scholarly challenges usually remain separate from the capitalist or corporate publishing system, which produces basic writing textbooks. Publishers (and the teachers who buy the books) often act as though multiple linguistic communities either do not exist or exist but must be transformed for their own good through remedial education, and especially the use of drill-and-skill models of correct language usage. Publishers often argue that they are "giving the customers what they want" by supplying these books, which is certainly true with regard to overworked two-year college teachers. They do so without reservation because they assume that market forces enable a wide range of buyers and sellers to find one another in a fair and open marketplace that creates choices through competition. However, recent developments in global capitalism have led one textbook editor to characterize the vision of the open market as limited by a "tyranny of the bottom line" (Silverman 1991). Publishers "represent" fewer titles in order to take fewer economic risks, and buyers have fewer less diverse choices available to them.

Assuming that respect for students' linguistic and cultural differences is desirable, we might ask whether a monolithic and increasingly global corporate publishing economy can adequately serve the needs of the diverse range of students we see at two-year colleges. I will attempt here to reinforce Silverman's point that current structural and economic developments and practices in the publishing industry make a diverse range of texts less available to students, but I will also argue that publishers could be involved in a more local and grassroots sort of way. I am not suggesting that the obstacles to change are not significant. Although editors and others are often well meaning and even knowledgeable about institutional and structural constraints, they may be unable to change their employer's system for publishing books and may see particular practices as unassailable, no matter how undesirable the outcomes of these practices may be.

School Publishing, Educational Institutions, and the Economy

Economic hardship in many parts of the United States has created an ongoing struggle over limited public resources, including resources targeted for education. All college and university campuses both contribute to and are often directly affected by these economic conditions. For example, on many campuses larger class sizes, due in part to unexpected enrollment increases, especially among part-time students who are often women or are older, affect the quality of education, particularly at two-year colleges (Gabert 1991; Craig 1990). However, declines in traditional eighteen- to twenty-four-year-old enrollments along with diminished state aid in many parts of the country led administrators to increased use of part-time faculty, hiring freezes for full-time faculty, and layoffs linked to budget cuts, all of which made large classrooms more common (Grassmuck 1991; Gordon 1993; Nicklin 1994). Throughout the 1980s and into the 1990s, students, in turn, faced rising tuition rates (Evangelauf 1986; Gordon 1993). Although tuition in some two-year schools is finally stabilizing,[5] many educational institutions continue to maintain revenues through tuition hikes while increasing administrative control over students and faculty/staff. This is often accomplished by increasing administrative hires and salary increases while simultaneously privatizing services that lower overall costs and reduce the quality of education received (Pew Higher Education Research Program 1990; Leatherman 1991; Chaddock 1992). Costs to all college students have gone up, class sizes have gone up, and some services have gone unprovided as those with the least power (students and low-status teachers and staff) bear the brunt of the cutbacks. Those with the most power have consolidated their control and protected their interests.

As consumers, college students dealt with their diminished purchasing power by putting pressure on publishers; they purchased fewer supplementary course texts. This is particularly true for community-college students with less money to spend on books. Publishers have responded by investing larger amounts in basic texts, including texts on the web, which overworked and often part-time teachers then use to teach those overenrolled courses in ways that demand less teacher labor. In this way, the investment in basic texts benefits both teachers and publishers because large production and distribution operations make more profit from a single expensive product than many cheaper products. In terms of the overall quality of textbooks, however, the result is fewer titles and less diversity. A less-diversified investment portfolio means publishers then rely more on extensive market research and more direct involvement in production to target a bigger, more general readership and to protect a big investment. Publishers may also intensify their involvement in production through cost-saving efforts such as author-assisted books that require noted authors to write only part of a text or revise an existing text, while editors or others write the rest. Another cost-saving strategy is the managed text, written entirely in-house but reviewed by a noted authority who sells the use of his or her name to the publisher (Keith 1991, 47).

How Publishing Mergers Continue to Make Matters Worse

Publishers also like larger investments in fewer textbooks because they save more by achieving economies of scale in storage, distribution, and production. During the 1980s and 1990s, overworked teachers (especially at two-year colleges) relied more on textbooks to provide curricular instruction because of a lack of time and authority to create their own curricula. Institutional constraints that centralized authority for the purpose of "right-sizing" educational institutions, often at the expense of classroom instruction, intensified this dependence. Publishing mergers also attempted to centralize authority with equally negative consequences, including the establishment of economies of scale and associations with megacorporate interests (Rudman 1990; Greco 1989; Horowitz 1987).

Larger publishers would often buy smaller ones for their innovative or specialty products, but if innovations didn't pay off, smaller publishers could be treated like cash cows and drained of their assets as punishment. Even if smaller publishers were not punished directly for their lack of profitability, they might be directed or encouraged to produce a narrower range of products, so as "not to compete, overlap, or in industry jargon, 'cannibalize' one another" (Sewall & Canon 1991, 62). Even the threat of a corporate raid could lead to the downsizing of a company to fend off hostile takeovers. Bluestone and Harrison have shown that although mergers and acquisitions have characterized several historical periods, few rivaled the 1980s for size and number, especially publishing mergers.

This history is illustrated by the example of Time-Warner, which bought textbook publisher Scott Foresman in 1986, only to quickly sell it to Harper and Row, which later became HarperCollins. In the end, Time-Warner decided to confine its business interests to entertainment. Or take the example of the late British entrepreneur Robert Maxwell, who acquired MacMillan Publishing Company in 1989. MacMillan had only that year joined with McGraw-Hill and Merrill Publishers to overtake Harcourt, Brace, Jovanovich (HBJ) as the largest schoolbook publisher in the United States. Maxwell had been trying since 1987 to acquire HBJ, until 1989 the largest educational publisher due in no small part to its own acquisition of Holt, Rinehart and Winston from Columbia Broadcasting in 1986. HBJ had diversified its interests over the years by selling insurance and developing theme parks in Florida, but in 1987 it was forced to spend $2.5 billion fighting off Maxwell's takeover efforts. The only reason HBJ survived, even after it sold the theme parks, was because General Cinema offered to buy the company from bondholders, who, as one analyst put it, "presented an offer that was close to what they might receive in bankruptcy, but with a chance to cash out sooner" (Donnelly 1991, 32). In the meantime, MacMillan and other Maxwell subsidiaries suffered from the death of Maxwell himself in 1991 and the indictment in 1992 of his two sons for embezzlement. All of these textbook publishers provide materials to community-college classrooms, but few educators appreciate the business contexts that shape their priorities.

The View from the Inside: Bigger as Better

Given this history of fast-paced economic restructuring and other forms of right sizing in the publishing industry, how do publishing insiders respond when pressed to reflect on institutional changes? In my conversations with ten editors and sales managers representing a range of popular basic writing textbooks, most expressed little animosity about the relationship of their employer to its parent company, even though in one case an editor had been forced out of his previous job because of a corporate takeover. Editors and others stressed that even though the parent company might "call them to corporate accountability," they could also "bail them out" when times were tough because of uncontrollable factors like declining enrollments, at least until profits increased. They also stressed the profit advantages of an economy of scale that centralized printing and storage costs.

From the inside, defensiveness may seem natural, but an examination of how insiders' personal values affirm the values inherent in corporate restructuring reveals assumptions that deserve further scrutiny. Many practices and objectives that editors often accept uncritically as givens are reinforced by large-scale corporate operations, thus making a critical examination of any particular stage in the process of textbook production more difficult.

What sort of editorial attitudes and practices are legitimized by a corporate preoccupation with large-scale profitability systems? The primary objective stated by most of the individuals I interviewed was to "serve teachers." However, the ways they conceived of serving teachers raises questions about what *service* means. For example, much of the emphasis on serving teachers also emphasized *adaptation* to fixed classroom circumstances or to perceived teacher deficiencies. Editors of basic writing textbooks would sometimes justify the publication of generic sentence books or books focusing exclusively on sentence manipulation and grammatical correctness because, they said, teachers want premade homework assignments or because teachers must teach courses devoted entirely to sentence writing. These teachers were sometimes labeled "old fashioned" or "too lazy" to think up other activities, an attitude that focuses on individual blame at the expense of analysis of publisher's objectives.

Another editor argued that the popular text published by his company was designed to "get students through the course in a simple, step-by-step fashion that leads students through the process [of writing]." Beyond the now well-challenged assumption that a single, linear process exists for all writing students, this editor also assumed that a teacher's primary concern was for a text to simplify the material so that students would not lose confidence and drop out. The range of writing processes and objectives a student might adopt became less important when the objective of the textbook was limited to retention rather than to other purposes, such as the improvement of student writing.

Concern over retention is not new. Retention has been a primary objective of two-year colleges wishing to avoid the revolving-door syndrome first described in the 1970s (Richardson, Fisk, & Okun 1983). Retention is certainly a primary objective of publishers who are keen to see their books used up (that is, blanks filled in), so the books are less likely to appear on the used-book market. Similarly, publishers' interest in a step-by-step writing process serves publishers as much as teachers because the description of a single predetermined and mass-produced writing process continues to legitimize the role of publishers as primary curricular providers for writing teachers, making teachers more dependent on textbooks and less dependent on themselves or other teachers. Process as a concept is often ignored, reformulated as steps or procedures, mentioned briefly and then abandoned in favor of grammar instruction, or contradicted by text structure and emphasis on nonprocess concerns. Continued reliance on the publisher's texts to define curricula reinforces the general trend toward increasingly disenfranchised and disempowered teachers.

Another way editors solidify their status as curricular providers is through a review process that intensified as the publishing industry has become more centralized. The traditional methods of ensuring returns on investments are through marketing surveys, peer reviews, and ongoing visits by sales representatives and editors alike to both schools and professional conferences. Questions in the peer-review process focus on such issues as reading grade level, whether assignments work, whether the text is logically organized, and other concerns that are teacher, not student, determined. Content may also be eliminated if even a small number of teachers find something too controversial during a peer review. Peer-review questions are intended to produce books containing material that appeals to as broad a range of teachers and administrators as possible to enhance sales. However, when fewer publishers produce more of the same kinds of books, the need to broaden the book's appeal intensifies along with the competition, and the content of the book loses focus.

Some in publishing see this as an opportunity to deal with the "problem" of "variously educated students" by emphasizing a "centrist comprehensiveness, structured pedagogy, and lack of leading edge debate" (Lictenberg 1994, A48). Conflict is avoided and a lowest-common-denominator mentality prevails. We should not be confused by such reformulated back-to-basics language, however. When what is defined as basic is constructed in terms of what sells the most to the widest range of students, textbooks may become increasingly ineffective, not only because they are boring and unreal but also for economic reasons.

For example, creating texts that have a broad appeal can lead editors to add desirable content as well as eliminate objectionable material. According to those editors I spoke with, most individual reviewers suggest additions not deletions. Editors are then compelled to incorporate the new material because the standard wisdom is "Nobody ever bought a textbook for what you left out." The result is that, while textbooks may start out as perhaps two hundred pages, by the third or fourth editions they may be three hundred to four hundred pages long. This can be especially true for basic writing textbooks, which carry grammar and usage chapters along with them as though they couldn't be published otherwise. Bulkier books, however, may be disadvantaged in an economy of scale. One editor described the increasing resistance on the part of students over the past ten years to the increased price of textbooks, especially longer books that are more expensive to produce. Students may decide not to purchase a lengthy, expensive book chosen by their teacher and instead share with other students or photocopy necessary material. The review process can in this way draw publishers into the double bind of lack of desirable content on the one hand or excessive content on the other.

Textbook content can also be influenced negatively by outside forces such as testing mandates and demographics. One editor spoke of adjusting text content to City University of New York (CUNY) grammar tests. Another well-known and often-used basic writing textbook devotes considerable attention in its teacher's manual to aligning textbook content with items on proficiency tests used in Florida and Texas. One sales representative noted that his company's textbook included multicultural readings, not because they were important for their own sake, but because they were used "in the bowels of Los Angeles," where whites were a minority. A similar logic was voiced by an editor who explained that a particular textbook was more sensitive to gender issues, not because teaching gender sensitivity was important in English or writing classes, but because "there are more women than men teaching those classes out there."

Editors say they publish books that customers (meaning teachers) want, but this oversimplified perspective creates problems for everyone. Although satisfying the customer is a primary concern in business transactions, concern can be manufactured when parent companies look to lock in sales as far in advance as possible to meet the needs of an economy of scale. The preoccupation with customer (teacher) demand can mean other participants (such as students) don't contribute their views directly because it would involve extra time and effort.

Information gathered by editors through the review process can also mean their own contributions in the development of the textbook are downplayed, unless of course the book is a financial success, in which case they accept credit for grooming a particular author. Editors generally limit their role to one of intermediary or negotiator who resolves conflicts between teachers' needs and publishers' constraints. Thus, when books don't sell, publishers claim it is because teachers were obstacles to innovation or because they were kept from producing new and innovative materials in some way by the bottom line, not because the process of producing the book was inadequate. Rather than see themselves as *participants* in the process of book production, editors and others involved in creating and promoting books understand publishing increasingly in terms of profitability first and content second. They see themselves as players in a game in which they become either the beneficiaries of corporate arrangements or the victims of economic stagnation in higher education. Both of these perspectives control and limit what editors believe can be published for teachers and students, and they make it impossible to transcend teacher parochialism.

Editors Beliefs About Teaching Writing

Despite a tendency to downplay their own involvement in the production of a textbook, the basic writing textbook editors I spoke with led me to believe that their involvement is far from neutral. Most of them held strong beliefs about how writing should be taught. Some valued and published progressively inclined textbooks that emphasized the writing of essays over sentence work alone and encouraged peer criticism. Others were defiant and defensive toward anything that suggested change away from prescriptive grammar models. The editor of one popular basic writing textbook defended her book by asking me, "If you don't know grammar, how can you communicate?" and "Do you think 50 percent of eighteen year olds can write a sentence? Don't you think that's kind of a necessary skill?" No matter how much editors believed in the power of the financial bottom line and no matter how much they pretended to be objective, they also held and endorsed particular beliefs and values, thereby participating in the construction of the bottom line, not simply responding to it. In this way, they help to shape the range of choices from which teachers feel they must choose.

Although no one would suggest that editors, publishers, and authors (not to mention teachers) can do whatever they want as they create and choose book content, the accepted givens ingrained in corporate profitability logic can become a means of legitimizing existing arrangements and practices in the publishing cycle of a textbook, especially practices that limit the involvement of students. Those individuals who have the greatest status and power can restrict the types of conversations that take place and who will participate in those conversations. More than other participants, editors emphasized their connection to financial constraints, but because their involvement is participatory, not simply reactionary, a better understanding of those factors that construct the bottom-line equation and how they are assumed to add up may be one way for all those affected by textbooks to begin to reconfigure that equation and thereby rethink relations among publishers, editors, teachers, and students.

A Counterproposal

Contrary to the global capitalist thinking that dominates most publishing enterprises, writing and learning are more accurately represented as diverse, wide-ranging activities not necessarily reproducible from one community (or community college) to the next. This perspective suggests opportunities to resist, challenge, and reformulate both the authority of textbooks and the structure(s) that reinforce that authority. What makes the writing done by authors in textbooks appear to have value is the production structure that concentrates profits in very few hands. A price is fixed based on an assumption that the writing contained within the book will be meaningful to large numbers of individuals, no matter how diverse their backgrounds or experience.

One alternative to this model is to make use of and even commodify heterogeneous student writing in ways that dismantle those economic incentives that have contributed to the production of homogenized, lowest common denominator textbooks (see Fraizer 1993; Harris 1991; Sullivan 1989). Rather than search for an elusive content designed to offend no one and maintain sales, publishers might devise a production scheme texts representing the diverse views of students, with the goal of accommodating a wide range of editors and educational institutions. Rather than smooth over differences and diversity, publishers might embrace them in creative ways. Publishers and editors might reconfigure both their market profiles and production procedures by making different groups of teachers and students not just buyers of textbooks but authors as well. Students and teachers might work together as part of their class work itself to create textbooks that define a socially constructed, localized knowledge base, drawing on both their own experience and the work of others whom they seek out as they take responsibility for their own learning by writing what they learn in book form. In this way, authority might be dispersed in a potentially more democratized and cooperative manner and would challenge existing hierarchical and authoritative teaching pedagogies now supported by traditional textbook learning and the post-1980s publishing industry. Such a project would also contribute to the sense of community that is a part of most community-college or two-year college missions.

By collectively reclaiming authority over knowledge traditionally owned and legitimized by publishers, students and teachers would also help to redefine what publishers do. Instead of giving teachers and students what they want, other options might become available to publishers if more teachers and students were persuaded to want to do it themselves. One possibility is that publishers might serve as coordination-and-distribution centers assembling diverse and localized educational booklets or treatises written by individual schools or classrooms. These booklets might contain a wide range of interpretations, activities, arguments, and discoveries grounded in diverse and unique classroom settings. There would be less of a need to market these booklets nationally because many classrooms would be producing them (thereby reducing some storage and distribution costs). More importantly, this could mean more risks might be taken in terms of content than are currently taken in commercially prepared textbooks. Local production could also mean publishers would risk less in terms of any single product investment and save on shipping costs. Sales might be invigorated by the distribution of classroom-produced texts within a particular region. A conversation might develop between different learning communities, or even different community colleges, and the number of markets and sales might increase. Selected past texts of this sort could be used by new classes to begin their own unique construction and interpretation of knowledge, standards, and values in composition. The constantly changing cycle based on localized production would model and reconstruct more democratic social relations between all involved, while maintaining a broad market base and role for publishers as coordinators, advisors, and distributors.

These recommendations turn traditional student-teacher-publisher relations upside down because authority flows from students and teachers to publishers, not from authoritative authors and publishers to teachers and then to students. More importantly, these alternatives could produce more humane and impassioned learning, while simultaneously working to resist those industry practices intensified by the late twentieth century mergers and acquisitions. If profitability continues to be the bottom line for most publishers, this alternative suggests a low-tech, low-cost alternative that could provide possible financial incentives through production-and-development savings while simultaneously promoting social justice through the learning process.

Notes

1. Patricia Cross (1976) has argued that the concept of remediation dates as far back as the post–Civil War era.

2. Piland notes that as late as 1983, most states had no official or working definition of remedial education, mission statement, or pattern of funding.

3. No matter what term is used—*remedial, developmental,* or *basic*—it is the writer, not the writing, who will be labeled, judged and acted upon by someone with his or her "best intentions" in mind.

4. See Kochman 1981, Smitherman and Van Dijk 1988, Stuckey 1991, and Street 1984.

5. See, for example, the experience of the California schools in Gordon (1993) and Merl (1993).

Works Cited

Bluestone, B., & B. Harrison. 1988. *The Great U-Turn: Corporate Restructuring and the Polarizing of America.* New York: Basic Books.

Bullock, T., D. A. Madden, & A. C. Mallery. 1990. "Developmental Education in American Universities: Past, Present, and Future." *Research and Teaching in Developmental Education* 6(2): 5–21.

Connors, R. 1986. "Textbooks and the Evolution of the Discipline." *College Composition and Communication* 37: 178–94.

Chaddock, G. R. 1992. "Industry Becoming the Big Partner on U.S. Campuses." *Los Angeles Times* (13 December): E9, E10.

Craig, F. M. 1990. *Older Adults: Community College Students of the 1990s.* Diss. Miami, FL: Nova University.

Cross, K. P. 1976. *Accent On Learning: Improving Instruction and Reshaping the Curriculum.* San Francisco: Jossey-Bass.

Crowley, S. 1990. *The Methodological Memory: Invention in Current-Traditional Rhetoric.* Carbondale: Southern Illinois UP.

Donnelly, C. 1991. "Harcourt Gets Fresh Start in General Cinema Takeover." *Investment Dealers Digest* 57(Sl) (23 December): 31–32.

Evangelauf, J. 1986. "Anticipation of Another Round of Big Tuition Hikes Sparks Debate Over Why Costs Are Rising So Rapidly." *Chronicle of Higher Education* (3 December): 1, 30.

Fraizer, D. 1993. "Textbooks and Writing in the '90s: The Commodification of Process and What Teachers and Students Can Do About It." *The Writing Instructor* 12(3) (Spring): 134–43.

Gabert, G. 1991. "Community Colleges in the 1990s." Bloomington, Ind.: Phi Delta Kappan Educational Foundation. ERIC ED 331558.

Grassmuck, K. 1991. "Colleges Discover the Human Toll as They Struggle to Cut Work Forces." *Chronicle of Higher Education* 10 (July): 1, 25, 28.

Gordon, L. 1993. "For Professors, Teach or Perish?" *Los Angeles Times* (19 January): 1.

Greco, A. N. 1989. "Mergers and Acquisitions in Publishing, 1984–1988: Some Public Policy Issues" *Book Research Quarterly* 5(3): 25–44.

Harris, C. R. 1991. "Looking Back, Looking Forward; Catch Me A Poem." *Gifted Child Today* 14(1): 2–5.

Horowitz, I. L. 1987. "Monopolization of Publishing and Crisis in Higher Education." *Academe* 73(6): 41–43.

Keith, S. 1991. "The Determinants of Textbook Content." In *Textbooks in American Society,* ed. P. G. Altbach, G. P. Kelly, H. G. Petrie, & L. Weis, 43–59. Albany: SUNY P.

Kochman, T. 1981. *Black and White Styles in Conflict.* Chicago: U of Chicago P.

Leatherman, C. 1991. "Salaries of Chief Executives in Higher Education Found to Have Grown by 6% a Year since 1988." *Chronicle of Higher Education* (3 July): A11, 12.

Lictenberg, J. 1994. "Publishers, Professors, and the Importance of Textbooks" *Chronicle of Higher Education* (18 May): A48.

Merl, J. 1993. "Fee Hikes Scaled Back For Colleges." *Los Angeles Times* (23 June): A3, 14.

Nicklin, J. L. 1994. "The Layoffs Continue." *Chronicle of Higher Education* (4 May): A37, 38.

Pew Higher Education Research Program. 1990. "Policy Perspectives: The Lattice and the Ratchet." Philadelphia, PA. Trustees of the University of Pennsylvania: 2(4).

Piland, W. E. 1983. "Remedial Education in the States: A Study Sponsored by the National Council of State Directors of Community and Junior Colleges." Normal, Ill.: Department of Curriculum and Instruction, Illinois State University. ERIC ED 251 160.

Richardson, R. C., E. C. Fisk, & M. A. Okun. 1983. *Literacy in the Open Access College.* San Francisco: Jossey-Bass.

Rudman, H. C. 1990. "Corporate Mergers in the Publishing Industry: Helpful or Intrusive?" *Educational Researcher* 19(1): 21, 24–27.

Sewall, G. T., & P. Cannon. 1991. "The New World of Textbooks: Industry Consolidation and Its Consequences." In *Textbooks in American Society,* ed. P. G. Altbach, G. P. Kelly, H. G. Petrie, & L. Weis, 61–9. Albany: SUNY P.

Silverman, N. 1991. "From the Ivory Tower to the Bottom Line: An Editor's Perspective on College Textbook Publishing." In *Textbooks in American Society,* ed. P. G. Altbach, G. P. Kelly, H. G. Petrie, & L. Weis, 163–84. Albany: SUNY P.

Smitherman, G., & T. A. Van Dijk. 1988. *Discourse and Discrimination.* Detroit: Wayne State UP.

Street, B. 1984. *Literacy in Theory and Practice.* Cambridge UP.

Stuckey, J. E. 1991. *The Violence of Literacy.* Portsmouth, NH: Boynton/Cook.

Sullivan, J. W. 1989. "The Immortalization of Chief Quinaby." *Principal* 69(2): 22–24.

Welch, K. E. 1990. *The Contemporary Reception of Classical Rhetoric: Appropriations of Ancient Discourse.* Hillsdale, NJ: Lawrence Erlbaum. Associates.

Westbury, I. 1990. "Textbooks, Textbook Publishers, and Quality of Schooling." In *Textbooks and Schooling in the U.S.: The 89th Yearbook of the National Society for the Study of Education,* ed. D. L. Elliott & A. Woodward, 1–22. Washington, D.C.

5

The Business Metaphor and
Two-Year College Writing Instruction

Robert Haight

The two-year college is in the business of education. Promotional campaigns attempt to attract new students through radio and television advertising. Programs are targeted to emerging markets including on-site educational opportunities at businesses, retraining of workers for growth occupations, international course work aimed toward a global economy, and distance learning to bring class work into the home. In addition, classes that do not fill are canceled, classes in high demand see sections reproduced to meet the needs of the incoming students, and, true to the demands of a market economy, growing numbers of part-time faculty provide their temporary service for a fraction of the cost of their full-time counterparts. To administrators concerned with the bottom line in perpetually tight or uncertain fiscal circumstances, education is a competitive marketplace indeed. Therefore, assigning the terminology of business in their communication with college employees is an appropriate vehicle through which administrators address their concerns. They are, literally, in the business of education.

It is quite another matter when the language of business is used to describe the dynamics of the classroom, the teacher-student relationship, the methodology of instruction, and the assessment of learning. The business metaphor so frequently used by business leaders, school administrators, politicians, and some educators themselves is attractive because it creates the illusion of certainty where there is uncertainty, sameness where there is difference, objectivity where there is subjectivity. It subtly promotes compliance to the status quo, at least in furthering an acceptance of the traditional power structure and its corresponding hierarchies. It maintains students and instructors in positions of disempowerment, as if the constituents of education know so little about it they have little to offer in how it should be run. Instructors and students as conceived by the traditional use of the business metaphor tend to occupy positions of lower management or as workers, not as chief executive officers or board members or stockholders. However, conceiving of a business metaphor that relocates students and instructors into positions of authority still forces a set of terms into an environment in which the language obfuscates instead of clarifies and offers empty, unqualified terms to support dubious analogies. When describing the roles of instructors and students, methods of instruction and assessment of learning, and classroom dynamics and curricula, the language needs to reflect the complexities of the constituents and activities if it is to be meaningful and if it is to serve the educational community and the community at large.

The Student as Product

Because the business metaphor tends to reflect the composition and view of corporate business, the most traditional terms to describe students create a metaphor portraying the student as a product. The product metaphor mirrors the conceptualization of an industrial or manufacturing economy. Viewing students according to these terms, the student is manufactured by the educational institution he or she attends to be used by the customer at the end of the production line. The customer is the business that eventually hires the student. One of the assumptions of this metaphor implies that all the products will be manufactured in exactly the same way. Therefore, assessment can easily identify flawed products and manufacturers. The illusion of sameness projected by the student-as-product metaphor has ramifications felt throughout the various curricula of the two-year college. The metaphor results in whole staffs of instructors being directed to teach from the same course syllabus, use the same textbooks, plan identical lessons in the same number of class sessions, and use identical teaching methods. Through this uniformity, the expectation is that all students will demonstrate identical skills on the same assessment instrument. In addition, instructors can be evaluated based on student success or lack thereof, and a particularly insidious example championed by Karen Hodges describes that "as a byproduct of these deliberations some academic freedom a faculty member traditionally has had to develop a personal teaching style will give way to a certain uniformity of quality control" (1994, 179). According to Hodges, through the application of this metaphor, instructors could become interchangeable technicians running identical class sessions. Probably the most striking characteristic of the student-as-product metaphor relates to the inanimateness of the student, the total passivity of the student's role in his or her education. Education becomes something that is done to the student. The student has no input into or responsibility for learning. The validity or relevance of the course work is assumed by those for whom the student is being prepared. Dale Drake (1994), a two-year college instructor, writes of IBM's support of education reform:

> IBM is a corporation who (sic) is accountable to stockholders for fiscal performance. As the world continues to shrink, competition becomes more difficult,

affording us little time for luxuries often found in "a well-rounded education." The luxuries I speak of are classes that do not contribute to "productive workers." Example: a student who has taken a quarter of "The History of Rock & Roll" instead of a "Time Management" class offers little to an employer. Tomorrow's employers will be more demanding of institutions and will not buy your product if you're not putting the right components into it.

According to the grim terms of this metaphor, the student product should be directed as to which classes to take so that he or she can be manufactured properly until sold to the future employer. Moreover, if a student fails or leaves the class, there is a flaw assumed in the instruction that must be accounted for. As Hodges states, "the bottom line is that we will be held responsible for the success or lack of it of our former students when they transfer into four-year programs or enter the business world" (1994, 178). This shows clearly the extent to which faculty are disempowered. It is difficult to imagine the same expectations placed on physicians in the medical community, where oncologists might be evaluated not according to their treatment plans and their medical abilities but only as to whether their patients survive. Through this thinking, we might conclude that oncologists are poorer doctors than pediatricians, whose patients most often flourish. The inanity of this illogic appears obvious when it is applied to the empowered medical community, yet it has been a driving force in discussions of education reform.

The most attractive feature of this metaphor to its proponents appears to be in the supposed objective, definable data it generates. The mechanisms are set in place before the course's initiation. The route is established and followed without exception. Progress is easily documented. In fact, if accountability were the goal of education instead of learning, the student-as-product metaphor would offer a most efficient option. Where the metaphor is used, accountability—not educating students—seems to be the directing force of the program. One reason the business customers, as well as politicians, have promoted this view of education might be that it offers the greatest amount of control to those who do not inhabit the classroom. The role of education is solely to serve future employers.

Instructors are able to defend themselves against accusations of shoddy workmanship by using this metaphor as well. They can argue that because they have no control over the raw materials they are to fashion the product from, they cannot be responsible for lack of quality, as businesses themselves would never expect to thrive if they assembled their products from defective materials. The student-as-product metaphor effectively relieves instructors of responsibility for incapable students—if students have shown any kind of learning or emotional or social problems they will be quickly documented to void the warranty; consequently, instructors will often exert a greater amount of attention to gate-keeping, that is, keeping out students who might be underprepared or who indicate the potential not to fit in. The instructors learn to place themselves to an extent beyond scrutiny, and an impressive array of special programs and labeling of students flourishes. The pressure associated with the ideal of a standardized, flawless product continues to grind against the reality of the plethora of abilities, disabilities, desires, and difficulties students embody.

At a time when higher reasoning skills seem most in demand by the business customers at the end of the production line, the student-as-product metaphor seems a contradiction to today's marketplace requirements. The student-as-product metaphor served an industrial society well, ensuring that passive workers executed the directives handed down from above. In the information economy, however, the metaphor doesn't work, as business expects a work force to operate as thinking team players involved in all aspects of decision-making. The contradiction between a new economy that needs animate students in flexible educational settings who are learning to learn independently and an educational system that insists on standardization cannot be easily resolved. The student-as-product metaphor and its corresponding terms describe only a wish for homogeneity.

The Student as Customer

The student-as-customer metaphor has become popular recently, mirroring the shift in the United States from a manufacturing to a service economy. Students as customers purchase the product of education and do with it whatever their individual needs and desires dictate. For students who have been traditionally relegated to inanimate products produced for the business community, the student-as-customer metaphor offers a greater degree of empowerment. Students can choose what, in fact, they wish to know. Students decide which plates at the buffet they will sample.

One of the byproducts of this metaphor is in its shifting of a focus on determining student fitness and its corresponding concentration on assessment of skills to a focus on measuring student satisfaction with the product. As Mark Edmundson (1997) writes in "On the Uses of a Liberal Education as Lite Entertainment for Bored College Students," he reads evaluations of his instruction in which students write only about how much they "enjoyed" his class, where education as entertainment and a dumbed-down curriculum ensure customer satisfaction. However, on a more positive note, through the student-as-customer metaphor and its desire for student satisfaction comes a greater degree of individualized learning. Contract learning offers an example of how this metaphor is realized. One student might contract to complete 70 percent of the work to earn a grade of "C." Another might contract to finish 90 percent of the work to earn a grade of "A." Both students could be highly satisfied with the educational product they received, although they might have developed different levels of skills. Though extreme, one could posit that a student could be entirely satisfied with the product, having failed the course. Because the instruction is viewed as the product, its fitness cannot be assessed through student performance, as students may have chosen to forgo aspects of instruction they would be tested on.

It could be argued that the conception of the businesses that hire graduates as customer and the conception of the students as customer are both valid. However, if that is the case, exactly which customer is being referred to in the writing and speech using the business metaphor must be clarified. It is, more likely, a situation in which empty language is applied to describe elements for which better terminology exists. Furthermore, one could argue that these conceptions are to a certain extent contradictory for the responsible classroom teacher. For many instructors, delivering instruction without regard to assessing student skills but only to ensuring the student satisfaction as a customer seems bizarre, indeed. Similarly, insisting on a set of outcomes handed down from business or governmental power brokers who themselves may know little or nothing about education theory and practice without eliciting the desires of the students seems equally peculiar. The instructor now occupies a position of attempting to satisfy the student customer while simultaneously trying to serve the business customer that expects skills and attitudes the student has no desire to acquire. The instructor, then, must act as a mediator between two groups that rarely, if ever, have any contact, let alone dialogue, with one another.

The Student as Client

The student-as-client (and the instructor-as-consultant) metaphor—as the student-as-customer metaphor—is empowering to the student who chooses an expert (teacher) to offer education as a product. The student is then free to put as much time and effort into maximizing his or her investment as desired. The thrust of this metaphor is slightly different from the student-as-customer metaphor in that there is not as much emphasis on customer satisfaction without regard to customer performance. In this respect, the student-as-client metaphor places responsibility on the student to perform, and lack of performance is documented to illustrate that it contrasts with the student's investment objectives. Because the instructor is taking on the role of consultant, there is an implication that continual assessment of performance will occur with the student, complete with honest appraisals of strengths, weaknesses, abilities, and motivation. Again, because student objectives might differ, results in student achievement would have to be interpreted according to individual desires and needs and would offer reliable information on the level of entire classes or programs only based on average performance of similar groups.

As with the student-as-customer metaphor, the student-as-client metaphor tends to move away from standardization, implying different activities within the same syllabus, potential altering of content to reflect student interests and perceived needs, and calling for various methods between classes or between individual members of classes. The notion of the instructor as a technician applying a preconceived set of operations as implied by some management theories does not apply. Perhaps this more flexible view of instruction comes from the adoption of the metaphor in the writing center, which, free of the responsibility of grading student performance, limits its practice to consultation for the greatest possible benefit of its client (McCall 1994).

Implications of the Business Metaphor

The business metaphor as it is applied to education tends to use marketing and management terms in undefined, though rather predictable, ways. As Ley S. Smith, former president and chief operating officer of the Pharmacia-UpJohn Company, told a group of high-school teachers, "You can think of education as business, because it's all about customers. Students need basic skills and a positive attitude before they get to the work place" (Latora 1994, C2). One should wonder according to these terms who the customer is that he refers to, the student or the employer after graduation. As educators, we read about our products, not knowing if the education or the students are being referred to, about customers, not knowing if businesses or students are the referent. At times, the terms are so devoid of meaning they can be interchanged or offered as a mixed metaphor without skipping a beat, as Hodges demonstrates: "In this metaphoric view of education (the Community College as Business), the student is the customer and the college a business that will be held accountable if it produces a flawed product" (1994, 76). Is the student the customer or the product? Is the power holding the college accountable really the customer? Is it possible that the student could be both a product and a customer? If the student is both product and customer, are there areas of contradiction impossible for an instructor to satisfy? For example, if the instructor must ensure the product is not flawed, but by doing so guarantees a dissatisfied customer, to which entity does the instructor pledge allegiance? Because of its unqualified language, this metaphor suffers under scrutiny. But hearing and reading so much of this politicized language, we are often assaulted as teachers by business leaders or politicians telling us such things as "customer satisfaction is excellent. It produces a product that is both durable and attractive" (Regan 1988, 49) and we are left to wonder what, if anything, is meant. Although some students might be considered durable and some attractive, it is difficult to conceive of either a student or of education as a "durable" and "attractive" product. Just what are those terms supposed to mean? What terms are typically not applied?

We do not encounter articles arguing that our students should be viewed as stockholders, the instructors as chief executive officers, the administrators as clerical workers, and the businesses themselves as stocks the students might eventually want to buy into or not, depending on *their* performance. We do not read that education is a gift, that it is a trade between instructors and students, that it is a vision quest. The business metaphor as it is applied to our educational institutions almost always leaves business itself beyond the scope of a critique. The *Chronicle of Higher Education* once ran an article whose headline was

"Business Should Be Run Like A Good University." Michigan Attorney General Frank Kelly stated, "It's almost disrespectful to be against corporations, as if they are some sacred grail, that they are the holy source of all our freedom. God help us if we have to depend on a corporation to get our freedom" (quoted in Channing 1998, D1). When we are told that we should run our classes more like businesses, an examination of meaning should occur. If we are to run our classes like businesses, does that include downsizing our student population to include only those who will be most productive, who will give us—the teacher as business executive—the best numbers at assessment time? Should we become accustomed to high failure rates, accepting them as a reality of the enterprise? Should we recruit and then select only those students who reflect our values and authority (those who display a positive attitude)? If two-year college classrooms were to operate like businesses, the same fractionalization and stratification would likely take place in our institutions as have taken place in our communities as a result of our current means of doing business. Our current means of doing business with its lack of commitment to workers in part necessitates the existence of the two-year college, offering hope for the dispossessed, laid-off, and underemployed.

Implications for Writing Instruction

The business metaphor as applied to the classroom limits the student-teacher relationship in that, to a certain extent, the closeness of the human interaction is deemphasized as individual personality, values, mythologies, and world views are sublimated for the more homogeneous culture of the corporate environment. Traditional terminology, such as the terms *apprentice* (beginner, disciple, pupil), *master* (teacher, guide, mentor), *tutor* (trainer, coach, instructor), *professor* (teacher, educator, instructor), and *student* (scholar, beginner) seem to possess as an aspect of their character a connotation of humanism and guardianship. Terms associated with the business metaphor, *customer* (buyer, user, purchaser, shopper) *product* (output, result), *client* (consumer, customer, user), and *executive* (capitalist, baron, mogul, magnate) connote a limitation of the relationship to exclude empathy on a personal level, an understanding vital to the learning process. As William McCall states, "Consultants, who are most noticeable in business settings, seem colder, more interested in problems clients are either experiencing or trying to avoid than in the person or people who face the problems" (1994, 167). Of course, many businesses in recent years have worked diligently to establish a climate that shows concern and care from their highest ranking executives to their smallest customers. But it is easier for most to associate Total Quality Management (TQM) to businesses rather than TLC. "Business ethics," the old example of an oxymoron, didn't become a sarcastic cliché because it was unrecognizable. Because the classroom is, or ought to be, a sanctuary for students, our discussions of the classroom and its inhabitants should reflect the highest standards of tolerance and concern that translate into professionalism in the educational field. Teachers need to be proponents for their students before they become gatekeepers for some illusory constituency that is rarely defined in the diverse terms in which it exists.

Teachers of writing, perhaps more than others, have the responsibility to act not only as guardians of students' rights to be different but also as stewards of language itself. As experts in language usage, it is the responsibility of writing instructors to insist on the clear use of words, to articulate the possible agendas connected to the use of certain kinds of language, and to clarify the conflicts inherent in the demands for standardized usage. Hodges writes:

> Many in higher education, and particularly those in the humanities, object to considering colleges "businesses" and students as "clients." But like it or not, more and more administrators, governing boards and state legislators insist on viewing us in this light. . . . While we in the humanities may resist the thinking that reduces students to customers and what we do to profit-motivated production of goods, we cannot deny the existence of such viewpoints. (1994, 177)

This proposition implies an acceptance of the terms offered, that the instructors mentioned have no authority or responsibility to critique the language used, to analyze the veracity of the metaphor, and to offer possible interpretations and subtexts. In contrast to this acceptance of others' language to describe the teaching-learning process in the writing classroom, one would think the responsible writing instructor would make it a subject of discussion with students and business and governmental leaders, analyzing the terms and metaphors proposed and offering other possibilities that may have remained unheard. The difference between the standard of English expected by proponents of the business metaphor and language usages of many of the more dislocated students from that standard puts students into an adversarial relationship highlighting their difference from the power structure whose dialect the standard represents and often fueling a loathing for the intricacies of their own language patterns. Irene Vasquez describes the conflict between business writing, her Mexican American family, and herself:

> Writing has always belonged to Them. When that writing entered the family domain, the instinctive reaction was to close in, to protect, to hedge your words. Whatever the writing said, it always signaled a threat. This writing did not dissimulate. It was a direct expression of power. Writing was always coming in from the outside: bills, taxes, insurance, court papers, school notices, and I, it seemed, at a certain age, was always leaving the family domain when the writing came in to go out there, to speak, to translate, to interpret *los papeles* for my mother, for my grandmother, an uncle, aunt, to protect the family from the ominous possibilities of the writing. Later, after I left home to get an education, *los papeles* were often the organizing principle controlling the timing, purpose, and quality of home visits. *Los papeles* continue

coming in and exerting this power. We all take turns, brothers and sisters, going home to deal with *los papeles*. (1994, 9)

Often the gatekeepers will assert that the standard must be learned, internalized,
and practiced because that is what will be expected in the business world. Expected by whom? In what business world? The business world is moving inexorably toward a composition of the many diverse elements in society worldwide.
The reality is that the standard is not standard, but that language and acceptable
usage are shifting, evolving, mutating, and acting as alive as language's users.
Still, it is not uncommon to happen upon a situation such as this: A commit-
ted writing instructor in the two-year college asserted that although an African
American student could prepare thoughtful, well-organized papers, he still had
dialectal "flaws" on the in-class writing assignments and therefore had been told
to drop the class because there was no chance of passing. In these circumstances,
the metaphor is quite clear and ownership of the language is indisputable.

As leaders and experts in the field of language usage, teachers of writing
should be available to challenge the often-misinformed beliefs about writing
and language held by many of those in the business and governmental sectors
—those whose decisions impact the writing classroom. When articles appear
showing some executive's top-ten list of writing errors—relating to such pri-
orities as copyediting concerns—writing teachers need to respond with the current expertise of the discipline to move these novices toward a more-informed
view of the complexities and subtleties involved in the whole of the writing process. Writing teachers need to be visible in instructing the business and governmental leaders about the cultural relativity of language usage and organizational
patterns in writing so that as their work force and clientele change as the culture
changes they don't assume when they read writing foreign to them in some ele-
ment of usage or method they are seeing something incorrect. In short, they need
to be instructed that the thesis at the beginning of the essay isn't correct, it's Eu-
ropean, that when a Japanese business letter begins with images of the beauty
of the season it isn't missing the point. The writing teacher of the twenty-first
century will need to be an expert in various rhetorical patterns and language usages and will need to act as an instructor to both students and the students' even-
tual employers, bringing both to informed opinions about language use and mediating the many differences among diverse populations across the community.

To play such a central and expanded role in education, writing instructors
will need more freedom to teach to individual differences, not less. Assessment,
which will continue to be a significant component of the classroom dynamic,
should reflect the learning and instruction rather than determine it. Skills assessment should take place within a larger context of assessment, including
student input, methodological assessment, instructor self-assessment, and peer
review. Although institutions should track the retention of their students, the
notion that an English teacher who "loses 25 percent of her English composi-

tion class . . . will be expected to document the losses and develop a plan for reducing the dropout rate" (Hodges 1994, 179) puts instructors in a position of continually justifying their competence from data unrelated to their teaching effectiveness, reducing the potential for experimentation and innovation as the tried-and-true, instructor-directed class takes its place as the sole method of instruction, not because it is the best method of instruction but because at most it is easy to document and it at least does not generate conflict. What changes will the instructor make to lower the dropout rate if students left because they found they could take an easier or more entertaining course? That they did not wish to be required to attend class? That they wanted less work? Retention statistics are important information for an institution to record, but the connection between attrition and class quality is spurious and management practices related to quality control hardly apply in this arena. The instructor should keep track of instruction and student performance, adjusting the curriculum to individual student needs and desires while challenging students to grow. The conflict in the expectation that an instructor will produce flawless products and the expectation that an instructor will have 100-percent retention is unresolvable in reality but easily imagined by the business metaphor.

In the two-year college, we currently do not practice much in terms of assessment of methodology. We have remained silent as we have been told we will be assessed as instructors solely by the results of student performance. Student performance should be one aspect of professional assessment. Too often, however, this type of assessment implies that all our students are equally motivated to learn, to listen in class, to attend class, to read material at home, and to accept the instruction we offer. Very little attention is given to whether we use methods considered in the profession to be state of the art, whether our knowledge base is up to date and exhaustive, and whether we are professionally engaged and active in professional organizations (Kroll 1994; McGrath & Spear 1991; Clark 1987). Little attention in the two-year college is paid to which teaching methods are promoted by the most respected members of the profession, to knowledge that goes beyond the pedestrian, or to the general reputation of instructors among colleagues and students. Evaluation of instruction rarely, if ever, focuses on instruction when applying the business metaphor. The idea of instruction as an art complicates its agenda of standardization.

As the Commission on the Future of Community Colleges (1988) suggested, the community is not only "a region to be served but also a climate to be created." We can approach the classroom community not as simply an area in a building with its regular collection of students buying and instructors selling but also as a climate to be created. Certainly some aspects of the classroom interaction are businesslike—just as a fraction of the life of a community involves business affairs. However, there is a great deal more: the cooperation of constituents, the caring and help of neighbors, the respecting of individual differences, the welfare of the group as a whole. As Wendell Berry writes,

Community, however, aspires toward stability. It strives to balance change with constancy. That is why community life places such high value on neighborly love, marital fidelity, local loyalty, the integrity and continuity of family life, respect for the old, and instruction of the young. It prefers to solve its problems, for example, by non-monetary exchanges of help, not by buying things. A community cannot survive under the rule of competition. . . . It is impossible not to notice how little the proponents of the ideal of competition have to say about honesty, which is the fundamental economic virtue, and how very little they have to say about community, compassion, and mutual help. (1990, 134–35)

If the classroom is to operate as a community, a sharing of responsibilities and power will inevitably emerge. Communities will develop different personalities, goals, and strategies to reach them, depending on their strengths and weaknesses. They will decide on the direction they wish to pursue and monitor how they are getting there. The business metaphor is so limited in describing classroom interaction and the roles of students and instructors it is really of no use at all. The time has come for the writing instructors to teach this to the community they serve.

Works Cited

Berry, W. 1990. *What Are People For?* Berkeley: North Point Press.

Channing, C. 1998. "Kelly Lashes Corporations, GOP 'Stooges.'" *Kalamazoo Gazette,* (17 May): DI.

Clark, B. R. 1987. *The Academic Life: Small Worlds, Different Worlds.* Princeton, NJ: The Carnegie Foundation for the Advancement of Teaching.

Commission on the Future of Community Colleges. 1988. *Building Communities: A Vision for a New Century.* Washington, DC: American Association of Community and Junior Colleges.

Drake, D. 1994. *Comments on Commcoll: A Discussion List for Community and/or Junior Colleges* (15 September): 196.

Edmundson, M. 1997. "On the Uses of a Liberal Education as Lite Entertainment for Bored College Students." *Her's Magazine* (September): 39–49.

Hodges, K. 1994. "The Future Community College Instructor as a Business Executive." In *Two-Year College English,* ed. M. Reynolds. Urbana, IL: The National Council of Teachers of English.

Kroll, K. 1994. "(Re) Viewing Faculty Preservice Training and Development." In *Two-Year College English,* ed. M. Reynolds. Urbana, IL: The National Council of Teachers of English.

Latora, A. 1994. "Portage Teachers Get a Business Lecture." *Kalamazoo Gazette* (27 August): C2.

McCall, W. 1994. "Writing Centers and the Idea of Consultancy." *The Writing Center Journal* 14 (Spring): 163–71.

McGrath, D., & M. B. Spear. 1991. *The Academic Crisis of the Community College.* Albany: SUNY P.

Regan, D. 1988. "Overcoming the Polyester Image." *Community, Technical, and Junior College Journal* 58 (February/March): 49–50.

Vasquez, I. 1994. "Verbal Privilege." A paper presented to the administration of Western Michigan University, Kalamazoo, MI.

6

Critical Literacy and the Politics of Technical Training

John Paddison

. . . In the tale of Sandford and Merton, where the two boys are described as amusing themselves with building a hovel with their own hands, they lay poles horizontally on the top, and cover them with straw, so as to make a flat roof: of course the rain came through: and Master Merton then advises to lay on more straw: but Sandford, the more intelligent boy, remarks that as long as the roof is flat, the rain must, sooner or later, soak through; and that the remedy is to make a new arrangement, and form the roof sloping. Now the idea of enlightening incorrect reasoners by additional knowledge, is an error similar to that of the flat roof; it is merely laying on more straw: they ought first to be taught the right way of raising the roof. Of course knowledge is necessary; so is straw to thatching the roof; but no quantity of materials will supply the want of knowing how to build.

I believe it to be a prevailing fault of the present day, not indeed to seek too much for knowledge, but to trust to accumulation of facts as a substitute for accuracy in the logical processes.

> —Richard Whately, from the
> introduction to *Elements of
> Rhetoric.*

Though written in the early nineteenth century, Whately's assertion provides a good deal of insight into the current educational dilemma of how to accurately define and describe literacy. This dilemma resides in our attempt to adequately determine the connection of reading and writing abilities to such concepts as functional literacy, cultural literacy, technical literacy, work place literacy, and critical literacy. I think that, when analyzed more closely, the anecdote of

Masters Sandford and Merton helps one to understand the truly interconnected, inseparable relationship of reading and writing, speaking and listening, to cognition and to learning, and, ultimately, to doing and to being. As well, one can begin to sense from this example the communal, collaborative nature of learning and human knowledge and can begin to appreciate the way in which language totally circumscribes human experience and social participation. Cognitive and linguistic processes go far beyond the realms of the mere application of better grades of information and more basic technical skills and abilities. True literacy involves not only the acquisition of knowledge—the knowing—but also the synthesis and responsible application of that knowledge—that is, the doing and the being. One needs not only to know what is right but also to do what is right based on that knowledge.

In a time when education is being shaken to its very pedagogical and theoretical foundations, when the ideological implications of teaching and learning are being severely scrutinized, Whately's vignette becomes particularly relevant. His brief but perceptive example illustrates the need for both teachers and educational theorists alike to reexamine how and by whom literacy is constructed. More significantly, especially within a critical context, is one very prominent question: In the broader American context, what does being literate truly mean?

More specifically, an area in education that would benefit greatly from such a redefinition and reconstruction of literacy would be in technical and vocational education, especially at the community-college level. For within this trade-oriented and skill-based area a good deal of emphasis is placed on the effective training of efficient workers for the job market—an extremely limited version of literacy.

Technical Literacy and Academic Margins

Given the origins, evolution, and mission of the two-year, postsecondary institution, there has developed a pronounced differentiation of expectations between the community college and the university. This differentiation is particularly obvious, I think, in a number of training programs prevalent today in many community colleges and their feeder high schools—programs such as Tech Prep (TP) and, more recently, School to Work (STW) projects, as well as more ill-defined programs like Total Quality Management (TQM). These are publicly and privately sponsored programs created solely for the successful integration of learners into the work force beyond the school. The purpose of such transition programs is to help noncollege-bound students prepare for initial participation in nonprofessional careers and for continued learning and development in the skill or trade areas that they have chosen. Proponents argue that the integration of academic and vocational curriculum within schools, as well as the linking of curriculum between high school and college, can build "stronger alliances with labor, business, and industry" (Wesson 1993, 198). By attempting to more closely relate school experiences to job or career experiences, such programs are necessarily a healthy reinvention of education. This type of educational restructuring is also held up as being meaningful and necessary for the two-out-of-three high-school students that have no desire to pursue a college degree (Lerman 1994, 20). To accomplish this end, these worker-oriented projects are constructed to make the school curriculum more closely reflective of and correspondent to the requisites of the working world, thus creating the need for specific work place literacies. Such fundamental reformulation of America's education system supposedly not only helps young people make a smoother transition from school to work but also strengthens their economic and citizenship participation. These programs are even touted as being critical if the United States is to regain superiority in the world trade arenas. At least that is the ideological sales pitch that seems to be most used by the advocates of such programs.

However, TP, STW, and even TQM can and should be viewed from a completely different, much more pragmatically negative perspective. Such a closer scrutiny would certainly reveal that the process of bridging of high schools and community colleges to the workplace necessarily links knowledge to merely "knowing and doing" in the teaching-learning process (Parnell 1994, 4). Of more significance, though, is the idea that such programs, in attempting to more totally permeate public-school and community-college curricula, recast a good portion of education into the marketplace model, with good teaching and learning being made analogous to effective training.

Many educators have come to the conclusion that these programs are merely a repackaging of those methods of social and economic control that so pervade existing education forms—that is, those age-old constructs of tracking and grading that have effectively sorted and categorized students since the inception of the American education system. In reality, innovative technical programs offer merely a fancier, more ideologically polished educational rationale for the systematic separation of the best and the brightest from those students with a propensity for the trades. The metaphor of students as potentially good workers that need to be trained or retrained, of students as good consumers of knowledge and information, leaves little room for the image of students as questioning, participatory, responsible human beings. Consequently, because the marketplace analogy of education is based on strong performance models of learning, much of the teaching that goes on within this context relies heavily on a pedagogy of positivistic-based, fact-oriented, value-neutral curricula and approaches, as well as on performance- or outcome-based assessment.

Based on this critique, educators have begun to question whether such programs will merely continue working to the disadvantage of a large segment of the society that is, was, and will continue to be placed at a disadvantage by the economics of the dominant culture.

The Politics of Technical Education

To support this critique, I would like to bring into this discussion a summary of what several contemporary educational theorists have posited about the lack of ethical and moral responsibility implicit in traditional, technically oriented educational contexts. The main critique by these theorists focuses on how the excesses and inequities inherent to the capitalistic free-enterprise system are transmitted and reinforced in and through education.

Theorists such as Balibar and Macherey (1987), Althusser (1986), Marcuse (1972), Bowles and Gintis (1976), as well as others, have accurately described how educational institutions reproduce capitalistic market relationships and ideologies. As such, schools become conduits for the sociological, economic, and political inequalities and power imbalances of the broader American capitalistic culture. This broader culture is one that is too hard-driven by greed and competition; this broader culture is one in which the hierarchies of inclusion and exclusion are subtly but sharply drawn along the division lines of wealth and nonwealth, white and nonwhite, male and female, and along the horizontals and diagonals of power and powerlessness, of equal and unequal, of justice and injustice. As well, in analyzing this broader American culture, educational theorists not only discuss how the realm of academia too closely mirrors the business world, but they also examine how educational practices stimulate, even facilitate, the ongoing reproduction of social and economic inequality. The language practices of education are instrumental in smoothly conveying to students the collective economic and social value and belief systems of the dominant cultural forms. These unanalyzed assumptions—which Michael Apple describes as "sets of lived meanings, practices, and social relations that are often internally inconsistent" (1982, 15)—allow a blatantly unequal society to continually legitimize and reproduce itself with little or no self-critique.

More significantly, these same theorists raise serious questions about the quality of the students who are being supplied to the broader culture by the assembly lines of education. Aside from obvious failures in such areas as minority retention and the teaching of basic literacy skills to *all* students, educational institutions have been criticized for producing uncritical, self-interested, consumption-oriented workers—those silent citizens who are most vital to sustaining a consumer-based society, a society whose chief purpose is to feed upon itself. Such theories help explain how education processes like grading and tracking very efficiently channel students into those long educational pipelines labeled "dropout," "technical/trades," and "college-bound"—paths that can often be either the open channels of access or the endlessly dark alleys of failure and desperation.

Certainly many of these theoretical constructs have been sharply criticized as being too atavistic and deterministic (Giroux 1983, 15–17). However, when the individual teacher considers the basic premises from which these theorists all work, reconciling educational theory to educational practice can and should become extremely problematic for him or her.

Given the number of critiques that have been made of the TQM, TP, and STW programs, the issue of agency is finally beginning to come to the forefront of the conversation. For example, in discussing the impact of such programs on college classes, Dale Clifford makes the following point: "It [the customer-driven model] is particularly useful for student services, the scheduling of classes, and registration. But the business metaphor can never encompass what occurs in the . . . classroom" (1994, 1). Additionally, as Richard Mendel has pointed out, such programs run the risk of perpetuating systems that maintain the "neglected majority" (1994, 10). Much more fundamental, though, is that such programs are subtle, very effective ways of silencing that neglected majority. Alfie Kohn makes the following assertion about such programs:

> [They fail] to address any fundamental questions about learning per se, or even more remarkably, curriculum. Incredibly, page after page, written by educators enamored of business models, typically contain not a single reference to whether the things we are teaching are worth learning—whether the curriculum is engaging and relevant to [students'] experiences. (1993, 60) I think that these critiques need to be taken a step further; I maintain that such programs, in reality, too often become very effective measures for using literacy against the learner. Much current theory discusses how power relationships are played out in the dynamics of literacy and language.

In discussing these power relationships, Giroux maintains that the dominance of an empirical-technical rationality in education creates a situation in which the status quo uses educational contexts for "control and certainty"—that is, pedagogy "which generates and supports behavior that is adaptive and conditioned . . . so as to ensure stability" (1985, 176). Such influences of stability and control have resulted in what Paulo Freire has described as the "banking" concept of education (1968, 59–63). As Freire maintains, this capitalistic educational model is one in that information is "deposited" in the student and "withdrawn" at a later time through objective tests, with a small amount of interest generated in the process. Within this educational setting, texts and ideas become merely inert artifacts that convey only received knowledge. Invariably, the dominance that knowledge and literacy have over students results in a systematic, ongoing silencing of those students, especially with regard to the contexts of the classroom. As Shor and Freire point out in their dialogues about education reform, such a teaching-learning environment openly declares itself "democratic" while actually constructing and reproducing inequality. The curriculum is presented as normative, neutral, and benevolent, . . . adjusting most students to subordinate positions in society. Inequality is presented as natural, just, and earned, given the differing "aptitudes" and "achievements" of various groups. The advantages of the elite are hidden behind a myth of "equal opportunity," while the idiom of the elite is named "correct usage" (1987, 121–23).

Deeply embedded in this model of the transmission of knowledge are dominant-subservient human relationships. Such relationships inherently allow little room for students to reflect on and question the dynamics and consequences of the processes that formulate and drive their very existences.

However, new studies in literacy are beginning to examine the way in which schools, through language learning, are able to convey the distorted valuation systems—those that invariably sustain class, racial, and gender stratifications. This passing on of unanalyzed assumptions through education and language practices is particularly obvious in the area of technical education, where knowledge and literacy are so easily treated as being merely skill based and therefore totally value neutral. Contemporary studies in critical literacy, when applied to programs such as TP, STW, and TQM help to peel back some of the facade under which these programs operate.

Critical Literacy as a "New Arrangement"

Critical literacy, when it becomes more of an imperative in the classroom, is perhaps the "new arrangement" that Whately called for in his analogy. Critical literacy, as a questioning-based approach to teaching and learning, is driven by an ethic of civic and social responsibility rather than by the ideals of capital formation, optimum return on investment, and profit maximization. Further, this classroom approach works against the skill and drill of performance-based education that is designed solely for turning students into effective workers, whose increased earning power makes them into more effective consumers. As such, a critical approach to literacy focuses on the differences and similarities between groups of human beings—that is, existential people, not drones or unquestioning automatons that are so caught up in a system of consumption that they eventually feed upon themselves. Finally, such an approach is, in reality, an attempt to understand the problems and conflicts that result in the social, economic, and political interactions among those groups of existential people. These problems and conflicts are, after all, the critical issues in life that go far beyond the worlds of school and work.

Therefore, I am defining *critical literacy* as the ability of students to use their own literacy skills to enable them to critically analyze and question the assumptions that they have formed about the broader communities in which they live. The teaching of critical-literacy abilities necessarily assumes that in any given learning situation the individual student can and will use language to promote a questioning, dialogic relation between himself or herself and any given context. This assumption contains a crucial dialectic between the individual and the context of the broader community in which he or she exists. For it is within this critical dialectic that students learn to question the greater ideological forces that are relentlessly exerted on them by the institutions of the dominant culture. Thus, if true learning is to take place, students must be given a voice with which to question those institutional forms and influences that too often serve only to divide and silence them. Only within this context does the critical dialectic provide all students—indeed, all people—with a lasting foundation for promoting social consciousness and participation and for the engendering individual responsibility.

Given the growing technical mission and function of the community college, however, and the subsequent emphasis on training, a fundamental contradiction is created. The concepts of critical literacy and technical education, in their present constructions, stand as contradictory terms, or even as binary opposites in a deconstructionist sense. For it seems that an economic system that has relentless competition as the driving force cannot afford to have questions asked about the methods and means that are used to attain corporate profits or business or industrial goals. How does one go about questioning the essential motives or methods of the very institution of which he or she is a fundamental part? The worker or citizen is never positioned to critique the excesses and the abuses of the free-enterprise system. Indeed, very few if any opportunities for true questioning or criticism are built into the existing economic institutions. Because there are infinite, well-placed mechanisms of silencing and complicity at work in the business world, any introduction of systems for critical questioning would be, under the present circumstances, less than openly welcomed and embraced.

Under these circumstances, the only thing that remains certain is the ongoing, persistent dilemma of agency with which the community-college teacher must continually grapple. If one believes that critical literacy is necessary for the complete student, how does one integrate this concept into technical contexts? If one accepts that a questioning perspective is a vital part of any curriculum, this acceptance goes far beyond the current exigencies of the two-year institution. At the community college, learning to be an emergency medical technician, a house builder, a secretary, or a computer technician is not necessarily synonymous with becoming a questioning, participatory, responsible citizen of a sorely troubled world.

Implications for Teaching and Classroom Practices

In the face of this dilemma, the process of critical reflection, even critical literacy, on the part of individual teachers must be paramount, especially for those who teach in technical contexts. Research suggests that classroom methodologies based on critical ethnography would do much to solve this dilemma. Using the approach of critical ethnography in the classroom allows both the student and the teacher to address the crucial questions regarding whose interests are really served in the classroom.

Anderson and Irvine (1993) describe critical ethnography as being the individual teacher's conscious search for question-based classroom methods—those methods that tenaciously search out the inequalities and the excesses of privilege that permeate, and are thus sustained by, the curricula and its delivery. This questioning search itself then becomes the paradigm for critical, reflective teaching and learning on the part of both student *and* teacher. Further, in applying critical ethnography to more specific purposes, Lankshear and McLaren maintain that critical ethnographers are able to use their own critical-literacy skills to identify the ways in which institutional arrangements and policies can contribute to illiteracy and inequality (1993, 28). Their work calls for increased individual, classroom-based observational studies that use critical-literacy skills in ethnographic studies, especially when students are the ethnographers. When one considers that critical literacy is a key component of critical ethnography, then the methodology comes into sharper focus. Critical, question-driven reading and writing provide student ethnographers with the access and means for the critiquing process.

An example of a classroom application of critical ethnography might be to have students do a critical observation of the schools that were responsible for their own literacy skills. Which students had the best literacy preparation? What was the economic foundation for those students that went on to universities? What are the dynamics of tracking and honors programs, and what are the implications? Another example might be a research assignment in which students do an extended ethnographic observation of a business or industry with which they are associated or hope to be associated. What are the economic and social goals—both stated and unstated—of that institution? What do the workers say about the organization, as opposed to what others within and outside of the operation say? What are the real and imagined assumptions about that company or industry that a close scrutiny might lay bare? A final example might be to have students question some of the unanalyzed assumptions and representations that are explicit and implicit implications of programs like TQM, STW, and TP. Whose interests are best served? What are the values and ethics that are represented and misrepresented? What are the direct and indirect costs and benefits of such programs? These, it seems, are some of the types of critical questions and approaches that might offer at least a possibility of critique and resistance.

Conclusion

By too quickly buying into programs such as TQM, STW, and TP, we as teachers risk also too readily promoting a detached, value-neutral version of knowledge within the classroom. Without analyzing and questioning the ideological assumptions that are at the core of such business- and customer-oriented models of teaching and learning, of literacy and education, we too easily come to see knowledge as being a stable, consistent, readily accessible body of information. In so doing, we inevitably deny the conception of knowledge as being socially constructed and power-laden and as being almost totally dominated and controlled by broader economic forces. Consequently, we also are cheating our students of the critical dialectic that provokes within them social consciousness and promotes individual responsibility on their part.

Of even more significance to me as an educator, though, is how these broader conditions and implications affect me as an individual—in the classroom. As Apple has pointed out, schools continually create and re-create the conditions by which ideological hegemony is maintained; therefore, ideological hegemony and dominance can probably be most obvious "in the day-to-day practices of individual institutions and [the individual] member"—the individual teachers, students, and administrators (1982, 40). Given this observation, I must continue to honestly question the rationale and assumptions—the agency —under which I work. For example, how can I move beyond merely turning students, as raw material, into the finished product of good, unquestioning workers? This is especially important with the growing popularity of objectified models of education that continually misrepresent the classroom as being analogous to the business site. With such persistent production metaphors, I can only ask myself if I am philosophically obligated to be the agent of an educational system that so effectively reproduces the status quo. If not, how can I serve as a catalyst to make schools the fundamental agencies for the social transformation of the human condition? Philosophically, what do I as an educator feel that students should not only know but also be able to do and be when they leave the classroom? Shouldn't effective teaching also be a search for what methods best serve to challenge and transform students and help them become ethically responsible, critically conscious, socially active agents of change rather than merely good workers?

Because such a large part of the community-college population is made up of people with working-class ties, perhaps what is needed is a new model of intellectualism for both teacher and student—the model of the working-class intellectual. Considering Antonio Gramsci's theories of the organic and the traditional intellectual (1972, 121), and Giroux's theories about the transformative intellectual (1988, 183), critical literacy and critical ethnography at the community college would seem to demand a revitalized model of teaching and learning. For within the framework of this new model, the working-class intellectual is concerned with how people, especially working-class people, come to more fully realize that using communication abilities for the critical questioning of their broader contexts is a fundamental precondition for life and living. Within this model, the potential for critical literacy is vital to all people, for such questioning dynamics are deeply concerned with the future of social, cultural, and political forms that embrace all people, not just a privileged few. This, I think, is the "new arrangement" that Whately suggests—that which goes beyond "merely laying on more straw."

Works Cited

Althusser, L. 1986. "Ideology and Ideological State Apparatuses." In *Critical Theory Since 1965*, ed. H. Adams & L. Searl, 121–35. Tallahassee: Florida State UP.

Anderson, G. L., & P. Irvine. 1993. "Informing Critical Literacy with Ethnography." In *Critical Literacy: Politics, Praxis, and the Postmodern,* ed. C. Lankshear & P. McLaren. Albany: SUNY P.

Apple, M. W. 1982. *Education and Power.* Boston: Routledge & Kegan Paul.

Balibar, E., & P. Macherey. 1987. "On Literature as an Ideological Form." In *Untying the Text: A PostStructuralist Reader,* ed. R. Young, 79–99. New York: Routledge & Kegan Paul.

Bowles, S., & H. Gintis. 1976. *Schooling in Capitalist America: Educational Reform and the Contradictions of Economic Life.* New York: Basic Books.

Clifford, D. 1994. "The 'Customer-Driven' Classroom: A Rebuttal." *The Teaching Professor* 8(9): 1–2.

Freire, P. 1968. *Pedagogy of the Oppressed.* New York: Seabury. Trans. C. St. John Hunter. New York: Seabury.

Giroux, H. A. 1983 "Ideology and Agency in the Process of Schooling." *Journal of Education* 165(1): 12–34.

———. 1985. *Theory and Resistance in Education: A Pedagogy for the Opposition.* South Hadley, MA: Bergin & Garvey.

———. 1988. *Teachers as Intellectuals.* South Hadley, MA: Bergin & Garvey.

Gramsci, A. 1972. *Selections from the Prison Notebooks,* ed. and trans. Q. Hoare & G. Nowell Smith. New York: International Publishers.

Kohn, A. 1993. "Turning Learning into a Business: Concerns About Total Quality." *Educational Leadership* 93(9): 58–61.

Lankshear, C., & P. L. McLaren, eds. 1993. *Critical Literacy: Politics, Praxis, and the Postmodern.* Albany: SUNY P.

Lerman, R. I. 1994. "Reinventing Education: Why We Need the School-To-Work Initiative." *Vocational Educational Journal* 69(3): 20–21.

Marcuse, H. 1972. *Studies in Critical Philosophy,* trans. J. De Bres. London: NLB.

Mendel, R. A. 1994. *The American School-to-Career Movement:A Background Paper for Policymakers and Foundation Officers.* Washington, DC: American Youth Policy Forum.

Parnell, D. 1994. *The Tech Prep Associate Degree Program Revisited.* Paper presented at the Annual Conference on Workforce Training of The League for Innovation in the Community College, New Orleans, LA, January 30–February 2, 1994.

Shor, I., & P. Freire. 1987. *A Pedagogy for Liberation: Dialogues on Transforming Education.* South Hadley, MA: Bergin & Garvey.

Wesson, L. H. 1993. "Vocational Education: Tech Prep." *The Clearing House* 66(4): 197–98.

Whately, R. 1828. *Elements of Rhetoric.* Rpt. by Carbondale: Southern Illinois UP, 1963.

7

The Politics of "Coming Out" to Colleagues, College, and Basic Writing Students

Leonard Vogt

Writing instructors invariably teach more than writing. To motivate our students and help them acquire enough information for essay assignments, we also often teach politics by discussing current events, by debating moral issues like abortion or euthanasia, by centering class writing around highly vitriolic national issues (WTO protests), or by asking students to relate their particular identities to issues of race, gender, or class. In addition, we also bring into the classroom our own particular views on these issues, although some instructors, I am sure, still believe that objective or apolitical teaching is possible. Students tend to like hearing their instructors' views on topics, as long as we present these views with an equal respect for our students' opinions.

Students watch teachers far more than teachers watch students. After all, they have one of us to observe and we have an ever-increasing number of students to observe in each writing class. As we constantly ask students to reveal themselves in the intricate process of writing, we also need, willingly or unwillingly, to reveal certain parts of ourselves as we help a class generate ideas for a writing assignment. If an instructor has an obvious identity based on race, gender, ethnicity, or disability, he or she may easily decide to contribute personal experience to the issues at hand in the writing class.[1] For other identities less noticeable or defined, such as sexual orientation, the instructor must "come out" before offering personal observations.

For more than twenty-five years, beginning with Peter Elbow in *Writing Without Teachers* (Oxford UP, 1973), composition theorists have made it clear that identity is an important component of composition. Unfortunately, the significance of gay and lesbian identity in the writing class, both for students and for teachers, has been missing. Recently, however, a number of essays, and one complete book, have included sexual orientation as an equally valid identity from which students write and teachers teach. Ellen Louise Hart's "Literacy and the Lesbian/Gay Learner"[2] critiques earlier composition theorists for not validating lesbian and gay presence in the classroom. In "Breaking the Silence: Sexual Preference in the Composition Classroom,"[3] five straight teachers describe their successes and frustrations incorporating sexual orientation into first-year writing courses. Harriet Malinowitz's landmark full-length study, *Textual Orientations: Lesbian and Gay Students and the Making of Discourse Communities* (Heinemann, 1995), joins composition theory and Gay and Lesbian Studies to show the importance of including sexual orientation in the writing class, for both students and teachers, gay, lesbian, or straight.[4] This recent scholarship shows that coming out and teaching writing are, if not always easy, compatible and certainly increasingly necessary.

I have been at LaGuardia Community College of the City University of New York for over seventeen years. I came out to colleagues within the first year because a role model had already presented herself and the English Department had a refreshingly open and nonprejudicial atmosphere. Two-year colleges sometimes, but not always, can have the advantage of greater liberalism than four-year colleges because the community college has been more recently opened and the faculty tend to be younger and more influenced by the tolerance of the 1960s. The students at two-year colleges tend to be somewhat older, have more life experiences, and have been exposed to greater variations of lifestyles than traditional students at four-year colleges. Many two-year colleges have mission statements to respond to the diverse identities of their students. Even if sexual orientation is not usually specified in these mission statements, the very absence of the mention of gays and lesbians can be used for political leverage.

However, I did not come out to all of my classes until the early 1990s. Coming out within the supportive environment of my department was one thing, but coming out to the college at large and the students in each individual class resulted from a combination of the politics of LaGuardia's Task Force on Pluralism, the Lesbian and Gay Student Club, and the Lesbian and Gay Faculty Association.[5]

In 1988, The City University of New York (CUNY) mandated a Task Force on Pluralism for all of its campuses. LaGuardia's Task Force began work in September 1988 and two significant events over the next two years made lesbian and gay faculty feel excluded from the efforts of the Task Force to be truly pluralistic. In a grant proposal written by task-force members in 1988, no reference was made to sexual orientation except in a quote from the college president. In September 1989, when the Task Force was offering training, both in-house and by outside consultants, our gay representative identified his "culture" as being "gay" and the rest of the year was spent debating whether a gay or lesbian culture should be included as part of a multicultural campus.

Although the Task Force was not yet sure of the validity of including gays and lesbians in a pluralistic campus, the students were. In 1988 and 1989 they tried to form the first lesbian and gay student group. Their posters, amply distributed and posted throughout the campus, announcing the date, time, and place of the meeting, were defaced or torn down within twenty-four hours. Graffiti such as "Freaks and Perverts," "Jesus is coming, are you ready," "Fags and Dykes," "KKK will stop the gays," "Get Dead," and "God shows you what he thinks of you—AIDS" covered the remaining posters. Although we expected some student hostility (an openly gay professor recently had received homophobic pornography in his mail), we were surprised by the virulence. We had helped the students choose a rather obscure room for the meeting so wary students might attend without much notice, but straight students stood at the elevators occasionally jeering and frequently gawking at the students looking for the room. About twenty-five students attended and they clearly wanted to discuss substantive issues like coming out to their parents and friends, gay and lesbian film, and having lesbian and gay speakers come to campus. Students signed their names, addresses, and phone numbers of a list of attendees, but the list was lost because the mother of the student who took the list home discovered the list contained names of gays and lesbians at her daughter's college and destroyed it. Therefore, contacting students for future meetings became difficult. In addition, certain events at this first student meeting were intimidating. Just as the student conversations began to roll, the student government entered with cameras and began to film the proceedings. Students barely ready to come to a meeting and hardly ready to appear on film froze as they received so much unnecessary attention. In addition, officially to form a Lesbian and Gay Student Club, and thus be eligible for student-government funding, at least ten students would have to sign up, which, in essence, would be coming out to fellow students. All these obstacles (the defaced posters, the homophobic students, the lost list of student names, the cameras, the signatures) prevented such a large and substantial body of students from returning for future meetings.

In September 1990, the conflicts between the Task Force on Pluralism and the lesbian and gay faculty came to a head. The Task Force had a panel on pluralism scheduled for opening sessions (two days of meetings before the semester began) but without a gay or lesbian representative. About six of the gay and lesbian faculty confronted the head of the Task Force in the hallway and asked her into my office to demand that a gay representative be put on the panel, which was to meet the next day. We got our representative. At the session, the panelists described how their identity shaped their perceptions of multiculturalism and how they might have been discriminated against at the college. When our gay representative outlined his own discrimination at the college, he explained how, after three years on a substitute line, he came out to his department and was fired.[6]

After the Task Force session, the Lesbian and Gay Faculty Association began meeting. In the winter of 1991, a number of us came out in the college newspaper, *The Bridge,* in an interview article. With photographs and office phone numbers in print, we were able to inform students that we existed and give some background on our organization. I remember one particular event after the newspaper interview, which helped me understand the value of coming out as a faculty member, especially at a diverse, pluralistic campus. I had just finished advising a student who said she read our interview in the paper. After a pause, I asked, "What did you think?" I honestly did not know if she would offer condemnation or approval. She said, "I like it," and I asked, "Why?" She answered that, as a black, lesbian immigrant from the West Indies, she had never seen in print anything that acknowledged the complexities of multiple identities struggling to understand which identity on any given day created the greater oppression. In her response, I found the chain that linked together the reasons for why I wanted to come out to all my classes, just as I was already out to my colleagues, my friends, and my family. We lesbian and gay faculty members were expecting our students to form a lesbian and gay club of their own, with only minimal guidance and little role modeling from us. Only when we felt excluded from the Task Force on Pluralism could we not only organize ourselves into a viable campus group but also become influential in helping students create and expand their own club and begin the work of educating the college, the Task Force, and our own students of the importance of lesbians and gays in a pluralistic environment.

Although I did not begin coming out to all of my classes as a recurring political act until 1991, on several earlier occasions I had gone into friends' classrooms as a gay speaker at both LaGuardia and other two-year colleges and these earlier presentations laid the foundation for my understanding of the emotional and political balance needed to educate students and myself during the coming-out process. The success of two of these appearances and the failure of the third alerted me to what would or would not work; what level of tension or strain I could bear; what change in awareness I could reasonably expect students to make; and what the most controversial, delicate, and annoying questions would be. The successes partially resulted because both the teachers had adequately prepared the students for a gay guest speaker by previous discussion of gay and lesbian materials within either a social-science framework or a literary discussion. In both cases, the students were given an objective introduction to lesbians and gays, and the students were better prepared to take advantage of the personal insights the speaker could bring. In the class that failed, the teacher had not put my appearance into a context that helped students understand that I was a valuable resource for their classwork. Instead, some of the students saw my appearance as a free-form forum where they could criticize or condemn me.

From these episodes as guest speaker, the successful as well as the unsuccessful, I began to formulate some of the rules and procedures I would follow later when coming out was no longer as an occasional guest but as a regular semester event. First, I would come out within the context of some class discussion that would enhance the students' work. I would come out after a teacher-student bond had been created so students would have to evaluate their homophobia against a person they had already accepted and whose teaching (hopefully) they liked and appreciated. I would make it clear that, although my coming out opened the door for them to know as much about gays and lesbians as they wanted to know, they must understand that my honesty is to better educate them and not to give them the opportunity to express their possible homophobia in an abusive way. Finally, I would try to transform the politics of coming out in the classroom to the teaching of writing as frequently as possible.

The most successful and thorough integration of coming out to my students with the teaching of writing has occurred in my basic writing classes. On several occasions I have used Sarah Barber's *Connections: Using Multi-Cultural Racial and Ethnic Short Stories to Promote Better Writing* (Kendall/ Hunt, 1991), a collection of short stories including U.S. and international literature, with an additional focus on gender, race, ethnic origin, disabilities, and sexual orientation. The second day of class I asked a student to read aloud from the preface so the students early understood that the short stories, which became the motivation for the writing of their essays, included a truly representative grouping. The preface says,

> These characters also represent a many-colored, multi-cultural tapestry of the human experience: a lesbian, a Japanese umbrella maker, . . . a black youngster, . . . a Chinese daughter, . . . a Native American youngster, . . . a differently abled mother, . . . a materialistic French woman, . . . a married man on the brink of acknowledging that he is gay, . . . an ancient black grandmother, . . . an Egyptian wife.

Mild nervous tittering filled the room when the student got to the words "lesbian" and "gay" and I ignored it because I wanted to refer back to the event later in the course when we read the gay short story and wrote the follow-up essay assignment. Before we got to the gay short story around week four (of a twelve-week semester), we already had dealt with gender, using Kate Chopin's "Story of an Hour"; race, using Alice Walker's "The Flowers" and Eudora Welty's "A Worn Path"; class, using Guy De Maupassant's "The Necklace" and Gayl Jones' "The Roundhouse"; and disability, using Carole L. Glickfeld's "What My Mother Knows." Because sexual orientation remains more sensitive and threatening to students than these other issues, I like to have students identify with a broader spectrum of oppressions before dealing with society's and their own homophobia. Students who have grown quite liberal and sometimes even progressive on issues of gender and race, and who have come to these awarenesses through an analysis of the politics of sexism and racism on their lives, still hold out on homophobia as a justifiable bigotry.

When we read the first gay story, "Michael's Towel"[7] by Richard Browner, I used the same class format as with previously discussed stories. *Connections* has four worksheets (vocabulary, character analysis, fact questions, and thought questions) accompanying each story as aids in helping students discuss, understand, and ultimately write about the stories they have read. In groups, my students compared their answers to these study questions and, in the case of

"Michael's Towel," rumblings about the story's content became evident, even as various members of the class put some of their study-question answers on the board. One male student wanted to change Michael's name to Michelle. A female student, every time she used the word "man" in referring to Rob, the story's main character, put quote marks around the word and drew a sad little face above it. I did not address these examples of indirect or direct homophobia over the story at the time because I wanted to allow the students to express their feelings about gays and lesbians freely before I came out to them.

As the discussion of the gay issues in the story heated up, students got beyond initial emotional responses and seemed to want a great understanding of the motivations behind the plot. In short, they became curious about the gay and lesbian experience and were ready to write about it. What they needed was information. I asked if they would like a gay guest speaker to come to class and field any questions they might want to ask a gay person. The response was a resounding "Yes." We decided the writing assignment should be an interview essay based on the guest speaker's responses to student questions.

First, the students needed to create a list of questions as homework in preparation for the following week's interview and I promised to do my very best to find a guest speaker on such short notice. The following Monday, the students had their questions ready, but I wanted them to have some time to compare and discuss their questions in groups and come with group, as opposed to individual, questions. I said the speaker was on his way but had called to say he would be about a half hour late (luckily, this class period was two hours long). In the meantime, I put students in groups to compile individual questions into group lists, thus eliminating repetition and encouraging broader questions about the gay experience. After about twenty minutes, I excused myself and said I was going to meet the speaker in my office and bring him immediately to class. I went to a drinking fountain, took a deep breath, and returned to the classroom alone. The students were putting the final touches on their group questions and looked up with anticipation. I said, "Our guest speaker is here," and pointed to myself. Faced with looks of incomprehension, I repeated, "Our gay guest speaker is here," and pointed again to myself. Mild pandemonium ensued. Some students said, "Nooooo," perhaps trying to remember what comments or remarks they previously may have made in earlier discussions of "Michael's Towel." Other students just seemed pleased with the surprise. A few students said, rather under their breaths, "I thought so." In another very lively section of this same course, two students had left the room while I was "finding" our speaker and had not returned in time to witness my coming out. That class enjoyed the whole process so much they asked me to repeat the entire surprise so they could watch the response on the returning students' faces. I was relieved that after preparing for this interview for almost a week, we were ready to ask and answer some questions in preparation for our interview essay.

I asked the six groups in class to take turns asking one question each. Because I had promised that they could ask anything, I was not surprised by the initial sequence of questions: (1) In gay relationships, and specifically in mine, who plays the man and who plays the woman? (2) Who cooks and who cleans? (3) What made you gay? (4) Doesn't the Bible say homosexuality is an offense against God? (5) Is it true that gays want to recruit young people into homosexuality? As silly and misdirected as these early questions were, and as ludicrous to have to answer, these are the concerns students often first have as they get a chance to explore gay and lesbian issues. Even though these first questions reveal all the typical ignorance and homophobia in America about gays and lesbians, students need to ask such questions and be given honest answers, all within the framework of a classroom environment and with the knowledge that their thoughts eventually will have to go on paper.

For lesbians and gays coming out to their classes or for straight teachers opening up discussion about sexual orientation, these initial questions will be repeated and must be anticipated and prepared for because they address three major stereotypes produced by homophobia: (1) gender is somehow violated between gay and lesbian couples; (2) homosexuality is a religious rather than a civil-rights issue; and (3) gays and lesbians form an army of recruiters who are a threat to our nation's children. By anticipating these stereotypes, and the very basic misunderstandings students at community colleges may have about gays and lesbians, teachers can come prepared with data to refute gender stereotypes (for example, the wide range of occupations, appearances, and interests of gays and lesbians), religious justification for antigay bigotry (for example, the fact that the Bible does not mention homosexuality and historically has also been used to justify the oppression of women and African Americans), and the fear that gays and lesbians are a threat to America's youth (for example, the fact that the overwhelming majority of abuse cases against children are by heterosexuals, not homosexuals).

By their second round of questions, students were making more substantive inquiries and even relating them to issues left over from our reading of "Michael's Towel." How did I first know I was gay? How did it make me feel? Do my friends know? my family? Why did I come out to my class? Now we were moving away from those initial questions about sex and gender roles, talking about the importance and problems of coming out, and placing the discussion at a much broader level of lesbian and gay oppression. In short, we were moving from the very private, to the personal, to the more abstract: the exact steps necessary in our progression toward writing essays.

As both I and my students relaxed into the question-and-answer mode, they allowed me more control over organizing the discussion. The student who had drawn a sad little face over the word "man" on the blackboard asked how I had felt when some of the students like herself said insulting or derogatory things about the gay men in "Michael's Towel." After saying, "Awful," I could continue with the way lesbians and gays frequently hear homophobic remarks, about how this makes coming out difficult for young people, and about how indeed this difficulty can be seen in the excessively and disproportionately high suicide rate among gay and lesbian teenagers. Students asked if I had experienced antigay discrimination, which gave me a chance to speak of gay bashing as the fastest rising hate crime in the United States. Inevitably, the question of gays in the military came up and opened the door to discussing the extent to which our society will punish gays and lesbians if we do not keep quiet.

By now, the students had many notes and ideas, but on a chaotic level that needed much more work before writing. I asked the students to call out all the things they felt they had learned from the interview. Again, they began with responses from their initial questions about sex and gender, but now they said gay and lesbian couples do not necessarily play gender roles, that most gays are not recognizable as gay; in short, that stereotypes abound and they were becoming aware of them. As I wrote the many student responses on the board, in the exact order in which they were coming from the students, they began to see that organizing ideas would be essential before any essay writing could begin. As they categorized the over fifty responses on the board, they came up with four basic things they learned from the interview: (1) the stereotypes about gays and lesbians, (2) the difficulties and rewards of coming out, (3) discrimination and increasing violence against gays and lesbians, and (4) the need for gays to be included in a pluralistic society. With these four categories in mind, they could begin to work on thesis statements and paragraph development.

I spend the most time integrating coming out to my classes with the creation of writing assignments in basic writing classes because these students are sometimes not only unskilled in the writing process but also in the process of understanding someone different from themselves. In composition classes, writing-through-literature classes, and especially in liberal-arts electives, students tend to have a more highly developed sense of writing about alternative lifestyles. However, this does not mean they are homophobia free; rather, it means their prejudices may not be as raw as beginning writers and they may not need to ask such fundamental questions as the basic writing students do to prepare for their interview essays. Again, as in basic writing classes, I come out in connection with what we are reading or writing about in class. An advantage to this organic approach to coming out is that I must always include lesbian and gay materials to set my own scene.

My composition classes, like my basic writing classes, center around gender, race, and class so that sexual orientation is seen against a backdrop of more universal oppressions. By the second week, we are reading and reporting on a series of gender readings from, most recently, Virginia Cyrus' *Experiencing Race, Class, and Gender in the United States* (Mayfield Publishing, 1993). Last spring, I assigned seven readings, each dealing with how gender roles adversely affect women and men. The eighth reading, Dennis Altman's "Why Are Gay Men So Feared?", made many of the same points the previous gender readings had made, but students were not responding with the same vigor. They clearly were not understanding, or able, or willing to admit the connections between how both women and gays and lesbians are a threat to the patriarchal order.

Earlier, they had given numerous examples from their own lives of how gender roles were socially created and how these roles influenced behavior. To be sure the students understood the Altman essay, I used it as a way of reinforcing essay structure: in groups, students found and analyzed the introduction and thesis statement, topic sentences with supporting examples, and conclusion. Students still were withdrawn, at which time I added my insights to the Altman essay by coming out to them. Immediately they responded to the essay by giving examples of homophobia in their own lives. One woman's gay uncle died after being stabbed twenty-seven times in a vicious gay-bashing incident. Another woman loved going dancing at the women's bars with her lesbian cousin because there they could "really dance" without being hassled by men. Later that week, a student came out to me in her writer's notebook. It was clear that my coming out helped students understand homophobia with the same immediacy they had understood sexism and gender roles. Best of all, there were no groans when I asked them to write a paper on sexual orientation.

In my writing-through-literature class, I use an anthology organized by theme rather than by genre.[8] The first theme is "Growing Up and Growing Older" and, last spring, I chose selections that illustrated how that theme was influenced by gender, race, or class. I also chose an excerpt from Edmund White's *A Boy's Own Story,* which depicts the conflict the teenage narrator feels as he grapples with his homosexuality. Although his highly graphic description of his friend Tommy's body indicates intense sexual attraction, the narrator feels these urges are unnatural and unhealthy. Instead, he dates the most popular and attractive girl in school, but feels his time with her is like being "in a movie." Rather than understanding how the narrator's conflict reflects homophobia's influence on "growing up," many of the students felt, or needed to feel, he was merely going through a "phase." It was time to look at the biographical information at the beginning of the excerpt. I asked what other books White had written and they noticed *Travels in Gay America.* Was Edmund White perhaps the narrator of *A Boy's Own Story?* Looking at his birthdate, I asked what decade White would have been a teenager. I asked how difficult being a gay teenager would have been in the late 1950s and, aside from several older students, no one knew. I told them, and we took a second look at the story through my experience. For the essay topic, sexual orientation now quite naturally joined the trinity of gender, race, and class as significant influences on the process of growing up.

In Art, Politics, and Protest, a liberal-arts elective course, I came out in the context of the AIDS quilt. After looking at *The Quilt: Stories From the Names Project,* an assemblage of photographs and life stories of the memorial for people AIDS has killed, we read a review of the book. In the review, which detailed the variety and range of people affected by the AIDS crisis, I used one particular testimonial as my basis for coming out:

> Some of the panels work as powerful graphic statements, but even the least sophisticated (perhaps *especially* these) are very moving. One man's striking fabric design is disfigured by a roughly scissored hole: his lover's parents

cut the last name out when he took them the memorial he had made for their son; now, as part of the larger quilt, it testifies to their fear as plainly as to his care.[9]

I confirmed that for gays and lesbians there is tremendous "fear" and "care" for how parents will respond when we come out to them. Now that I was out to the class, I felt like I had really joined them. When showing additional AIDS protest art, such as the documentary *Common Threads,* or even bringing in an ACT-UP speaker to show the highly controversial video *Stop the Church,* I could speak with an openness that merited student respect. Exam questions relating to art protesting homophobia or a museum-trip assignment on the history of Gay Pride marches in New York City no longer seemed strained, inappropriate, or offensive to the class. One student, in her writer's notebook, quite flattered me by writing, "And then, without blinking an eye, he came out to the class." If it were only that easy.

My community-college students learn more about writing and about life when I come out to them, but I am the true benefactor. Coming out is never a one-step process: Each time a lesbian or gay teacher brings that private part of life into the classroom, there are different possibilities for teacher anticipation and student response. Coming out to a class is a political act that takes the power of the teacher-student relationship and further decreases it for the benefit of both teacher and student. If the faculty member is lesbian or gay, she or he makes a very personal contribution to demystifying sexual orientation. If the teacher is straight, she or he adds one more, and perhaps currently the most controversial and politically energized, social issue to the student's consciousness. The study by Harriet Malinowitz, mentioned earlier, opens up the many possibilities a homophobia-free classroom can create.

With growing attempts by the religious right and conservative educators to roll back progress on including gay and lesbian materials in the classroom, it is more important than ever for lesbian and gay faculty, when they are ready and when it seems safe to do so, to come out to colleagues and students. Our politicians and school boards pander to the bigoted fears of our growing homophobic society. Several years ago, the New York Board of Education dropped gay and disabled persons as categories within its multicultural education program.[10] Political candidates make clear their antisex and antirace agendas as ways of garnering votes. The classroom is one of the few places to withstand these onslaughts against lesbians and gays and provide space for students to process their own homophobia through discussion and writing.

After a lengthy process of coming out to my colleagues, my college, and my students, I enjoy the pleasure and completeness of an openly gay life integrated into my professional life as a professor of English at a two-year college. Without the political struggle of the students who shaped the Lesbian and Gay Student Club and the faculty who subsequently founded the Lesbian and Gay Faculty Association, my process and progress in coming out would have been impeded.

Notes

1. I realize the shortcomings of identity politics, i.e. identifying political struggle exclusively through one's own political oppression, and do not encourage it except as a step toward a larger understanding of political issues.

2. In *The Lesbian in Front of the Classroom: Writings by Lesbian Teachers,* edited by Sarah-Hope Parmeter and Irene Reti. Santa Cruz: HerBooks, 1988.

3. In *Tilting the Tower,* edited by Linda Garber. New York: Routledge, 1994.

4. Malinowitz's book is also useful for new or seasoned teachers who are beginning to incorporate sexual orientation into their writing classes. She has chapters offering background information on the history of Lesbian and Gay Studies, the social-construction theory in composition, and liberatory pedagogy, as well as course syllabi and writing assignments, and four extended student responses to her courses.

5. I thank Lenore Beaky from the English Department and Mark Blasius from the Social Science Department for helping me recall the following sequence of events.

6. He fought and won the case. The next year he was given a tenure-track line and today he is tenured.

7. In the future I would use a different gay story. Because "Michael's Towel" is about a married man who realizes he is gay, the story offers more complicated issues than a class needs to deal with on their first encounter with a gay theme.

8. Annas, P. & R. C. Rosen, eds. 1993. *Literature and Society: An Introduction to Fiction, Poetry, Drama, Nonfiction.* Englewood Cliffs, NJ: Prentice Hall.

9. McHugh, H. 1988. "They Shall Not Go Nameless." *New York Times,* (July 31).

10. Newman, M. 1995. "Schools Drop Gay and Disabled as Multicultural Studies." *New York Times* (February 25).

8

Assessment as Political Definition

Who Speaks for the Underprepared?

Daphne Desser

"Who speaks for the underprepared?" This question was posed to me by Dr. Ed White, a nationally known expert on writing assessment, during a recent e-mail conversation in response to my description of my experience as a first-year writing faculty member at Pima Community College, where I confront daily the reality of assessment as a tool for political definition.

Who community colleges admit and how administrators and faculty define our criteria for admittance are inextricable from our perceptions and beliefs about the role of education. Our admission policies can either further the cause of social justice or preserve standards that are assumed necessary by those of us who can meet them. I believe that we can create responsible, efficient, and fair tools for the assessing and placing of our students, which are not elitist but that are egalitarian and can actually function as a means to track students in rather than tracking them out. By "egalitarian," I mean that a significant purpose of our assessment and placement practices can be to allow many developmental students access to higher education by creating classes that are specifically designed for their skill level. These classes give students the time, attention, and opportunity for success that mainstreaming or nonmandatory placement does not provide. When students are able to successfully complete developmental courses, they are more likely to stay in school. The completion of remedial coursework has been found to be positively correlated to student retention. (White 1994, 12)

However, my belief in mandatory assessment and placement as tools for social reform is troubled by many disturbing realities. A rise in popularity of elitist approaches to education, wariness about assessment practices from writing faculty who often see large-scale assessment as intrusion, and lack of sufficient financial support from administration to conduct efficient and fair assessment and placement are a few of the stumbling blocks. Still, I see these as challenges to be met and not as reasons to give up on assessment and mandatory placement as tools for social reform.

In reflecting on the recent rise in elitist stances to education, I am reminded of my high-school American history class, where I first heard de Tocqueville's warning that democracy would eventually lead to mediocrity. For more modern versions of this warning, we need only to look as far as our coffee tables to recent issues of *Time* and *The New Yorker:* "In an egalitarian environment the influx of mediocrities relentlessly lowers the general standards at colleges to levels the weak ones can meet" argues William A. Henry III, *Time*'s late theater critic (1994, 65). His treatise on how an "overweening egalitarianism has debased higher education," includes the following "modest proposal:" "Let us reduce over perhaps a five-year span, the number of high school graduates who go on to college from nearly 60% to a still generous 33%. This will mean closing a lot of institutions. Most of them, in my view, should be community colleges . . . , These schools serve the academically marginal and would be better replaced by vocational training in high school and on-the-job training at work" (65). There is some truth to what Henry says. There is a need for vocational training that is specific and market-responsive. There are people who could benefit from skills-oriented courses in computer-maintenance and allied-health fields.

The question, however, is when and where this training should take place. Henry's suggestion that this happen in high school ignores the large number of people who require training later in life. His suggestion that vocational training after high school be provided at the work place ignores the reality that many people who seek such training are unemployed. I argue that there is actually a great need for postsecondary vocational training that is currently not being met. Private technological institutions are too expensive for the people who could benefit most from them. Community colleges' curricula, because of unclear mission statements and a befuddled sense of identity, often do not respond well to market demands with training that is up to date and accessible.

Most offensive to me is that Henry's "modest proposal" fails to recognize that community colleges have other purposes beyond offering vocational education. One of the most important purposes of the community college is that it provides a way in to nonvocational jobs and universities for a number of motivated and intelligent students who are academically underprepared but nevertheless gifted. This is a purpose unique to the community-college system, and it needs to be preserved.

Like Henry's article, James Traub's "Class Struggle" in *The New Yorker* is skeptical about offering academic options to remedial students. Traub describes his experience observing a developmental class at City College. The protagonist is the teacher Rudi Gedamke, a former member of the working class, a German immigrant, and a soon-to-be-disillusioned Marxist. According to Traub's interpretation, Rudi is impassioned, bitter, amd despairing, and identifies to a dangerous degree with his students, but above all he is misguided in his original belief that his college skills class serves its intended purpose. At the article's close, Rudi is described as unable to extricate himself from a system that is not working. Traub thereby suggests that even City College's original supporters have come to question its efficacy.

Why the Elitists Are Wrong and Why I Agree with Them

The now-unfashionable egalitarian commitments that gave rise to the open-admissions policy at the City University of New York are similar in sentiment to the philosophical commitments that gave birth to the community colleges. In my view, the increase in the number of community colleges and their ever-increasing enrollments are an eloquent argument that they are responding to an educational need overlooked by the traditional university.

Perhaps I should reword that and write instead "educational *needs,*" for we have in our writing classes in community colleges a great diversity in our students. At Pima Community College, for example, we have students from Mexico, Japan, Bosnia, Vietnam, Guatemala, and Russia, most of whom are attempting to gain citizenship and exhibit all the drive and idealism of the new immigrant. All of them have writing skills that require remediation. We have Hispanic and African American students who are the first in their families to attempt college and who have not been academic successes in high school. Their writing is full of slang, misunderstandings, and linguistic peculiarities. We have older students who return to school after losing their jobs, after recovering from drug addictions, and after prison or prolonged hospitalization, and students whose writing has experience but lacks direction and confidence. There are many young women with small children who became pregnant at thirteen, fourteen, and fifteen and are returning to school for the first time. We have a few white students aged eighteen or nineteen, just out of high school, working thirty to forty hours a week whose parents cannot afford tuition at the university. They are often unaware that they have ideas worth expressing, and their writing can be the worst—blank or uninformed. In my writing classes, I have a diverse population with something in common; many of my students are at a disadvantage due to poverty, lack of previous education and opportunity, and language differences.

I believe that the continued growth of community colleges is a testament to the service they provide in offering social and economic advancement to the academically underprepared. In taking this view, I can be considered what Kevin Dougherty calls "functionalist" (1994, 124). Functionalists view the expansion of community colleges primarily as "animated by a desire to promote equality of opportunity on the part of a broad coalition of educators, university heads, and state and federal officials" (1994, 124). Dougherty argues that the functionalist approach ignores the significant impact of government officials who promote the growth of community colleges primarily out of self-interest. Community colleges are popular with state government, according to Dougherty, because they give the appearance of helping to maintain a healthy economy and mobilize support of voters, both of which are necessary for reelection (1994, 125).

Whether Dougherty is correct in questioning that real social advancement exists for the academically underprepared through community-college education or whether Henry and Traub are correct in suggesting that we ought not be offering social advancement for these students at all become idle questions for me when I think of the students who come to my office. When I think of Carlos, for example, who once saved his life by flashing the right gang sign. Without the community college, Carlos would be either violent or hopeless. Without the possibility of a community-college education, however flawed, I fear that the students from the lower classes will either return or turn to welfare, gangs, or lives of crime. In Arizona, my home state, we have recently spent $4,304,944 on the justice system (census of state and federal correctional facilities; U.S. Department of Justice, Office of Justice Programs, Bureau of Justice Statistics, 1988) versus $612,468 on public institutions of higher education (U.S. Department of Education National Center for Educational Statistics, "Financial Status of Institutions of Higher Education 1991–1992"). The marketability of a community-college degree—how effective it is in serving as a bridge to the university, whether it instead veers students away from four-year universities who would otherwise attempt a university education—all become secondary concerns when I consider what other options are available to my students. Mike Rose has a wonderful passage in his book, *Lives on the Boundary,* that illustrates the significance of looking beyond the numbers to the lives of individual students.

> Attrition may be a blessing, as many contend, for it naturally purges the university of those who don't belong, those who never should have come. There's a kind of harsh institutional truth to that, I suppose, but to embrace it, you'll need to limit your definition of achievement; blunt your sense of wonder. What you'll have to do, finally, is narrow your vision of the society you want to foster. (1989, 204)

The faith that Rose seems to maintain for the future of individual, underprepared students is the same faith that inspires me to continue teaching basic writing despite the critiques of the institutional effectiveness of community colleges. The critics of community colleges are not entirely misguided, however. Open-admissions policies make it more difficult to create regularized, effective, and suitable curricula. The community college is attempting to cover too many bases right now; it offers vocational education, a cheaper, easier alternative to the university and a catch-all support system for minorities, the disabled, working adults, and other nontraditional students.

The community college will need to define itself more narrowly. I see assessment and mandatory placement as necessities in helping to define the future missions of community colleges—and this is where I find some common ground with the elitist perspective. Henry argues: "What America needs is not a fusion of the two tracks (vocational and academic) but a sharper division between them." (1994, 65). The instinct to track students is a good one, and I'm not sure why many of my colleagues, who share my commitment to education as a tool for social justice, as well as many prominent writers in our field, such as Jeannie Oakes (1985) and Mike Rose (1989), think that assessing and mandatory placement will, more often than not, result in unfair treatment to the students. Rose's well-known account of his experience as a vocational student, "I Just Wanna Be Average," details the hazards of tracking:

> Entrance to school brings with it forms and releases and assessments. Mercy relied on a series of tests, mostly the Stanford-Binet, for placement, and somehow the results of my tests got confused with those of another student named Rose. The other Rose apparently didn't do very well, for I was placed in the vocational track, a euphemism for the bottom level. (1989, 24)

Rose describes most of his experience as a vocational student as uninspiring, and his description of his boredom is often used as an argument against tracking. The problem with this argument is that it overlooks a significant part of Rose's tracking experience; his scores were mixed up with someone else's. Of course he was bored; he was never supposed to be in classes that moved at a remedial pace. But other students, students whose scores have not been mixed up by a strange administrative error, those students can and do benefit from courses that are designed to operate at their skill level. Teaching to a student's ability does not necessarily mean a lowering of the standards. The standards can still be high for that particular learning context. However, the context needs to be appropriate to the student's previous educational background and academic experience.

Assessment as a Tool for Social Reform

I am not advocating classes for developmental students that talk down to the students but imagine instead classes specifically designed for such students that incorporate Bartholomae's vision of writing classes that begin with what the students already know and bring to class. In this framework, the teacher comes to the class with respect for the students' knowledge and abilities. To Rose and Oakes, I would suggest that it is not tracking that they find so objectionable as it is tracking that is poorly done and in the wrong spirit. Teachers, students, and administrators have often assumed, mistakenly, that developmental students cannot be expected to be pushed in the same way regular students are.

In his book, *Developing Successful College Writing Programs,* White describes the lack of faith in fair assessment practices as a widespread phenomenon:

> Those who favor assessment are often from off-campus and are suspected by many faculty of association with political and economic interests intent on

> preserving discriminatory economic and social structures who see themselves
> acting on behalf of the less privileged. (1989a, 89)

I got my first dose of this nonsequitur (tracking means discriminating against the disadvantaged), when, as an adjunct faculty member, I spoke up at a Writing Department faculty meeting. The issue was whether we should designate first-year composition courses as prerequisites for upper-division literature courses, a mild form of tracking, because this would mean that students who had not fulfilled the first-year composition course would be excluded from such courses as Major American Writers and Women in Literature.

"But of course!" I blurted out, before I could stop myself, "if the students can't write an organized paper with a controlling idea yet, how are they going to attempt literary analysis?"

The head of the department nodded in agreement. A long-time faculty member did not: "This goes against the open-admissions policy that this college was founded upon!" he bellowed, as he stormed out of the room.

Nevertheless, the motion passed.

This story illustrates how the writing program at Pima Community College, despite protests invoking the spirit of open admissions, has become increasingly more open to using assessment and placement as tools for running our Writing Department more effectively. I believe that grouping students by mandatory assessment, when it is done well and with sensitivity to the students involved, results in more effective curriculum design and classroom teaching that is more suited to the individual students' needs.

Every semester, for example, I have a few students in my classes who have bypassed the entrance exam and want to try Writing 101. Often these students are international or students who have language difficulties. They are attempting to avoid the ESL courses or the Writing 70, Writing 75, and Writing 100 courses. Those students never do well in Writing 101. Some manage to scrape by, but over the years I have come to believe that they are better off starting in the remedial courses where they can do well. They can then always go on to Writing 101, Writing 102, or even the honors sequence. My purpose in recommending that they begin with the remedial course is not an attempt to track them out of the educational system but rather is an effort to keep them in it.

The developmental courses we offer at Pima Community College are similar to the regular writing-course sequence. For example, Writing 100 asks the student to write a number of essays with increasingly complex rhetorical situations. Writing 100 is not a skills or grammar course. It makes many of the same intellectual demands on its students that Writing 101 does. The difference? Not in the standards, the grading, or the students' native abilities, only in the students' academic preparedness, which causes those students to be uncertain or silent in regular classes. In developmental classes those students speak more, question more, and can excel.

My argument for tracking students into developmental courses is my attempt to keep them in school. I hope that these students will build confidence and gain knowledge in the remedial courses, which will give them a better background to work from when they take the regular or advanced first-year composition courses. Grouping by mandatory assessment would make my job of placing and subsequently teaching, each individual student easier. I could then develop curricula that do not need to encompass a wide range of abilities, skills, knowledge, and previous background levels (as I often do now). Instead, I could design writing classes that are more responsive to a particular group's needs. This does not mean that my expectations for the developmental students have been lowered. It means that I believe they will need more time and attention until they can catch up with students who are at an advantage because of previous academic experience.

At Pima, we now have entry and exit criteria for all our writing courses. We have held onto our holistically graded writing-sample method of assessment, despite recent fears that we might be forced by new state legislation to use a multiple-choice exam. None of these developments came easily, however, and we have a few more battles to fight. What follows is a brief history of the most recent changes in our Writing Department's decisions and an explanation of how the egalitarian-elitist debates are played out in our policy-making.

Trials and Errors: The Story of Assessment at Pima Community College

In the Spring of 1989, Dr. Ed White visited the Writing Department at Pima Community College. In his report to the provost he recognized the following strengths: the level of concern and interest in reexamining assessment procedures on the part of faculty and administrators, the use of a direct writing sample, and the practice of mandatory assessment. He saw the faculty's perception that the content and interpretation of assessment process had slipped out of their hands as the department's chief weakness. He also raised questions about test placement and how attuned it was to the curriculum. He also suggested that the holistic writing sample be continually revised and that faculty be consistently involved in the review of assessment procedures (White 1989b).

Dr. White's report is significant in that it suggests ways in which an egalitarian approach to mandatory placement and assessment could be made efficient and practical. First, he recommends that writing faculty be intimately involved with assessment procedures and practices; they should have the necessary information to carry the appropriate measure of responsibility. The reality is that if the faculty do not oversee assessment practices themselves, this power of overview will be taken away from them altogether. Faculty are much less likely to be supportive of an assessment practice that is designed by the administration, the state, or an outside regulatory agency.

Second, the report reveals a strong commitment to the academically underprepared. Assessment practices reflect how we recognize our populations. If we don't mandatorily place students in a developmental class, we cannot know how many students could benefit from the course; we don't know how many more sections of that particular course we should offer. The report also showed sensitivity to the needs of students who are immigrants and who are the children of immigrants. To not place the students, or to let the students choose which writing course they feel they can manage, does not help them. In fact, it offers them a less-effective education. Many of the students are not functionally literate in their first languages either. They manage through the regular writing courses largely by being silent and by picking up whatever they can, often not following most of the class discussion and the writing assignments, let alone being able to complete the assignments well. The average writing instructor is not trained in the identification of specific ESL errors and does not ordinarily have the time to give the student the extra attention he or she needs.

Yet this is precisely the type of at-risk student community colleges were designed to help. Wouldn't such a student be better off in a course specifically designed for his or her needs? If this is tracking, so be it; it is neither discriminatory nor elitist. It is offering students the most effective classroom teaching suitable to their specific needs.

Assessment as Intrusion: Why Faculty Are Wary

To oversee the assessment process fairly and efficiently, the faculty needs two things: time and money. Both are rare commodities in the community-college system, and without the administration's explicit financial support and support in time release to oversee assessment procedures, redesign placement exams, and continually update faculty on developments, the process cannot be handled equitably and responsibly.

White has argued that for writing assessment to operate successfully, the faculty need to be continually involved in the testing procedures, as well as rewarded, supported, and evaluated for their efforts. He suggests that "when teachers are involved in the testing of writing, the tests are likely to be much improved and the teaching will be improved by what participating teachers learn" (1989a, 104). Unfortunately, at the community-college level, complete faculty involvement in the development, design, and implementation of assessment and placement procedures is impracticable. Writing faculty rightly complain that teaching five classes of twenty-seven students leaves them little time or energy for keeping informed about large-scale assessment, let alone for being actively involved in its development.

Overburdening community-college writing faculty with large teaching loads of mostly developmental courses results in both ineffective large-scale and classroom assessment, which in turn negatively impacts the quality of teaching. In the classroom, writing teachers are expected to teach developmental courses but are often not given the resources to do this well. The classes are too large. This encourages teachers to assign fewer papers, to comment on papers more briefly, and to limit the number of individual conferences and revisions.

For developmental students, this truncated process is especially damaging. The faculty are aware of this and feel that they are not giving their students a real opportunity to learn. They feel sorry for the students, whom they see as fellow victims of a less-than-ideal learning situation, and they are, in response, often more lenient in grading.

In addition to large class size and heavy teaching loads, the diversity of the community-college writing students makes in-class assessment complex. In one classroom, there is often an enormous variety in talent, interest, experience, knowledge, cognitive abilities, commitment, cultural background, reading histories, language preferences, grammatical awareness, and writing skills. This diversity often leads to faculty frustration with establishing standards. The easiest solution is to not accommodate for the differences while grading. The combination of a diverse population, large classes, and the freedom of most community-college faculty to design their own grading systems create a situation where reliable and valid classroom assessment seems very difficult. Most of us are not up to the challenge and find ways of decreasing our responsibilities in grading. We invent creative rationalizations; grading is an unfair burden to the teacher because it is too subjective, it causes students to be inappropriately dependent on outside evaluation, it reinforces notions of competition and individualism, and it disrupts the teaching process. Perhaps the real reason is that the community-college writing teacher is often put in an untenable situation to do effective classroom assessment and is tempted, mistakenly, to avoid it as much as possible, rather than addressing the outside factors that make good grading so difficult. Large-scale mandatory assessment that is sensitive to the diversity in community-college writing programs would lighten the teacher's load by creating classes that are still diverse but less chaotic.

Making the workload of the individual writing faculty member more reasonable would allow faculty to develop and maintain a large-scale assessment program that is more reliable and valid and can make effective classroom assessment more feasible. In-class assessment is affected by numbers; I know this from my experience moving from teaching two classes a semester as an adjunct faculty to teaching full time. As an adjunct faculty member, I could create in-class assessment practices such as frequent conferences, revisions, and in-class exercises that I am no longer able to use with the same frequency given my current teaching load.

Many community-college faculty feel their first responsibility is to the students and not to developing departmental policy. Their focus is classroom centered; rather than looking at the structural conditions that help to create the difficult grading load, many writing faculty become immersed in learning how to cope with the numbers of papers that require their attention. We need an apparatus in which faculty members' less grading loads, teaching situations, and other assessment concerns can be periodically reviewed by a few representatives of the faculty. We need a vehicle with which we can continually remind the administration that treating the faculty well is our most valuable tool in keeping both in-class and large-scale assessment accurate and thereby ensuring the efficacy of our writing program.

The most significant structural change that needs to take place at Pima Community College, and probably at many community colleges, is the creation of a Composition Board and the development of a Writing Program Administrator position. This would allow concerned writing faculty the time, the money, and the vehicle for staying continually involved in large-scale assessment. For the rest of the faculty, it would allow an easier mechanism for staying educated about assessment procedures. It would allow testing practices to remain in the hands of the Writing Department, decreasing the amount of friction and the possibility for misunderstandings with the administration. It would provide a vehicle for ongoing departmental review, faculty discussion about both in-class and large-scale writing assessment, and a means for cooperation and understanding about assessment procedures. It would give the Writing Department responsibilities in assessing and placement the public recognition they deserve.

Assessment has too many wide-ranging political implications to be done haphazardly. The efficacy of the Writing Department depends on the accuracy of the assessment program. By far the most compelling argument for a renewed focus on assessment is that the basic writing program, when it is properly run, can be a powerful tool for student retention. As White points out in his studies of the California and New Jersey writing programs: "There is a clear, positive relationship between completing remedial writing and staying in college" (1993, 12). Especially at the community colleges, where we offer underprepared students a chance at academic survival, we need to make sure that our large-scale placement and classroom assessment are accurate and effective. Under the present circumstances, this is not possible.

Directions for the Future

Community-college writing programs offer many underprepared students a way into a more meaningful, functional life. Despite all the difficulties mentioned, community colleges continue to successfully offer associate in arts degrees, which lead to increased job opportunities; community colleges are also becoming increasingly sophisticated in providing a nurturing, more personal alternative to the first two years of a bachelor of arts degree at a large research university. Beyond these measurable successes, community colleges continue to offer people encouragement, a community of information seekers and learners, exposure to a wide variety of ideas, and the opportunity for reflection and intellectual growth. These are ways in which the lives of community-college students are made more meaningful and functional, but they are not easily measured.

To critics of mandatory placement and assessment, I suggest that poor implementation of tracking is elitist and discriminatory, but that does not mean by default that all tracking is. In the situation that Rose describes, for example, the teacher was not sufficiently prepared to teach developmental students. For some elitist teachers, the poor results of badly implemented tracking confirms that developmental students "don't belong; can't make it." But if these teachers were to go into their classrooms with more egalitarian attitudes, seeking to draw on the students' strengths and really believing in the students enough to devise a challenging and motivating course, then students could use the developmental writing class as a springboard to future success.

To ensure our survival, community-college writing programs need to be self-critical about how successful we are in offering the right writing skills to people who need them. The use of proper large-scale and in-class assessment has the potential to revitalize community-college writing programs and make them much more effective. Many of the elitists' criticisms about the ineffectiveness of developmental writing programs have to do with structural conditions that do not allow the teaching of developmental writing to be as productive as it could be. Changes, such as mandatory assessment and placement, the creation of Composition Boards and appointments of Writing Program Administrators, and ongoing faculty involvement in assessment practices could allow for much more effective classroom and large-scale assessment.

The political ramifications of our decisions about assessment—both as individual teachers in our classrooms and, collectively, when we make decisions about large-scale assessment—are tremendous. That these are responsibilities riddled with complications and contradictions does not mean they should be ignored.

Some of my students recognize the political aspects of assessment intuitively.

In a recent Writing 101 class, I discussed the process of writing this paper.

"What is it about?" my students asked.

"Well, it's about how our placement exams affect who gets to go to college and who doesn't," I responded. "For example, who we admit to WRT 101—and why—is a political decision." "That's stupid," one of my young white American students answered. "You just take the test. If you pass, you're in. Politics has nothing to do with it."

"No way," my Hispanic students replied. "How come so many of us are in WRT 100 instead of 101?"

"What if we didn't have WRT 100 or WRT 70? How many of you would be in college then?" I asked.

"Miss," one of my students hesitated. He is a young Hispanic male who is usually very quiet in class, the first of his family to attend college. In a conference with him earlier in the semester, I was taken aback by his attentiveness. I was explaining a grammatical rule halfheartedly because usually this type of information needs to be repeated. I looked over at Eli and realized he had been listening very intently. He then summarized in his own words exactly what I had just told him. "Thank you," he said, "I never knew that. But now that I know, I won't ever make that mistake again." He never did. This student was listening to me that intently once more. He asked me, "This paper? Is it going to be published? In a newspaper or something? Because I would like to read it."

I smiled. I didn't know about it ever being published, but at least my paper was going to have one interested reader.

"I'll make sure I get you a copy," I said.

Eli, this one is for you.

Works Cited

Bartholomae, D. 1985. "Inventing the University." In *When a Writer Can't Write,* ed. M. Rose, 134–65. New York: Guilford Press.

Davidson, A. 1994. "Writing Assessment Consultancy Report for Pima Community College" by Dr. White. Tucson. Unpublished. (November).

Dougherty, K. 1994. *The Contradictory College: The Conflicting Origins, Impacts, and Futures of the Community College.* New York: SUNY P.

Freire, P. 1988. *Pedagogy of the Oppressed.* New York: Continuum.

Henry, W. III. 1994. "In Defense of Elitism." *Time* (29 August): 63–72.

Little, J. A., & J. Carter. 1992. "Final Report on Multicampus Writing Assessment Project." Tucson. Unpublished. (Fall–Spring).

Montes, F. 1989. "Response to Ed White's Consulting Report." Tucson. Unpublished. (November).

Oakes, J. 1985. *Keeping Track: How Schools Structure Inequality.* New Haven: Yale UP.

Rose, M. 1989. *Lives on the Boundary: The Struggles and Achievements of America's Underprepared.* New York: Free Press.

Shor, I. 1986. *Empowering Education: Critical Teaching for Social Change.* Chicago: U of Chicago P.

Traub, J. 1994. "Class Struggle." *The New Yorker* (19 September):76–90.

White, E. 1989a. *Developing Successful College Writing Programs.* San Francisco: Jossey-Bass.

———. 1989b. "Writing Assessment Consultancy Report to Pima Community College." Tucson. Unpublished. (March).

———. 1995. "The Importance of Placement and Basic Studies: Helping Students Succeed Under the New Elitism." *Journal of Basic Writing.* 75–84.

9

On Being Nowhere

The Politics of Technology in Community-College Writing Classrooms

Mark Harris

"Seventy percent of success in life is showing up."

—Woody Allen

In cyberclassrooms, how do you know when a student's hand is raised?

It's official. The Information Age is here.[1] Saying so is news of the "dog bites man" variety, but we're only beginning to realize the implications of its arrival.

Not that we'll get time to adjust. Digital technology will continue to get smaller, faster, and less expensive: It is something of a truism that we get twice the power for half the cost every eighteen to twenty-four months. We haven't plateaued. This rate of change will continue and may even increase. After all, most of the essential concepts of our current technologies date back almost fifty years. What will machines, tools, and devices based on new concepts look like? We can only imagine how they will function and what changes they will produce in our lives.

What these shifting technologies will mean for society is a topic so enormous it staggers the imagination. Our employment, our recreation, our personal lives all will change in response to new machines that disappear into the fabric of our lives. Articles in newspapers and popular magazines tout the arrival of inventions and not-so-long ago touted as a kind of science fiction dream: wearable microprocessors and nano-robots that perform surgery.[2] High-definition television (HDTV) is certain to hasten the fusion of telephony, Internet and entertainment technologies. Xerox's "What's the difference?" ad campaign, which highlights the similarities between digital documents and paper ones, might apply here too.

Like every other aspect of our culture, education is changing as a result of the pressures and opportunities brought about by these technologies. This chapter will focus on the impact of Information Age technologies on the tools and society[3] of higher education, with particular attention to the community-college English composition classroom. My goal for this discussion is to paint with broad brush strokes: to suggest directions and trends without going into too much detail. Revolutions are by nature unpredictable in outcome, and my observations are tempered by a dozen years of working in networked environments, both virtual and face to face.

The Death of Print

The Information Age is proving to be a good thing for reading and writing. While we await the triumph of the digital text—like Mark Twain's death, news of the end of print has been "greatly exaggerated:" newspaper, book, and magazine sales continue to climb—e-mail, chat rooms, and discussion groups are helping to reestablish reading and writing as fundamentally important human activities.

Some of the best writers in college classrooms today honed their skills posting to Bulletin Board Services (BBS) and newsgroups, and the World Wide Web is a fertile arena for spoken-word poets, limerickists, and erstwhile travelogue writers.

The universe of electronic texts is working other changes as well. In networked classrooms, the teacher's voice is one of many, and the usual deference shown to the teacher as an authority figure is absent. The power dynamics of face-to-face classrooms have evolved over centuries. They are so familiar to us we hardly have to think about them. Teachers have power, while students, by and large, do not.

In virtual classrooms, however, students can share in what once were exclusively the teacher's prerogatives: access to information, ability to broadcast messages to class members, the possibility of conducting small-group and even one-to-one discussions in the midst of the large group.

Like much of the change associated with technology, these changes are mixed in their effect. The sharing of power once concentrated in one person, the teacher, would seem to be a good thing from a variety of perspectives, but teachers and students in some schools complain about the change. Teachers ask to have control of the network returned to them (check out the number of software packages patterned after the network-management software used in business, especially those that allow teachers and managers to monitor and even censor what students and workers can do with the network). One teacher even asked if it weren't possible to turn off the Internet in his networked classroom during his course periods.

Students sometimes feel more comfortable learning from a single, authoritarian information source than learning to navigate, analyze, and assess the multiplicity of sources available from the Internet or even the campus net. However, these tools are fundamental to learners, workers, and citizens of the Information Age.

These tools allow easy access to massive amounts of information; shifting power relationships are central to the digital revolution and will shape education as drastically and strongly as they will shape society itself. It is impossible to say with certainty what the outcome of this process will be, but even at this relatively early stage, some principles are emerging as dominant.

The Role of Community Colleges

Because of the large number of community colleges and the huge variety of communities they serve—from industrial to rural—it is risky to generalize about them. Nevertheless, public, two-year colleges are both incubators for the twenty-first-century work force and a proving ground for democracy in a global capitalist economy.

Schools are one of the primary social institutions for the promulgation of culture,[4] and community colleges have filled an especially interesting role in this regard, extending the democratizing and leveling impulses of K–12 education (in the United States, anyway) into the rarefied atmosphere of the academy, with its ivied walls and ivory towers. With one eye on an elitist tradition and the other on the changing needs of their local service areas, community colleges have always suffered from double vision. In our era, the pressures of our rapidly evolving society are blurring their vision even more.

Writing Classroom: Community College = Community College: Society

Community-college writing classrooms are curious places, in part because they reflect all the tensions and competing influences of the colleges that contain them. First-semester writing classes in particular enroll almost everyone who attends a community college. They are one in a small (and diminishing) core of common courses often known as "general education."

Since the middle of the twentieth century, writing classes at public, two-year colleges have served a variety of functions in addition to the teaching of writing. Everything from basic study skills to library competency has at one time or another been blended with the introduction to composition. It should not surprise us, then, that at many community colleges, writing classes have been among the first courses (outside of computer science and data-processing courses) to integrate the use of computers.

Computers make writing much easier, removing the burden of rote copying and making formatting a paper to any requirements easy. Introducing computer skills early in a curriculum also makes good sense and, at many schools, computer instruction in writing classes became a sensible alternative to the ill-conceived computer-literacy courses that blossomed in the early 1980s.

There have been costs to this use of the writing classroom as a point of first contact; some believe that the first-semester writing course has lost its focus and retains few ties to the rhetorical traditions that it inherited. This double view extends to nearly every area of our lives touched by technology, and it has been said that the dawn of the Information Age offers us two equally possible scenarios. One is the Dystopian view sometimes associated with cyberpunk: a high-tech, low-life society where a handful enjoy the benefits of secure, long-term employment with vast, multinational corporations, while the rest of us struggle to live by our wits using a variety of sophisticated technologies to limp through our lives.[5]

There is another, rosier view, no less likely than the Dystopian view, for all its optimism. This view, sometimes known as the Global Village,[6] presents a society spanning the planet, where the digital revolution continues the trend of the industrial revolution, making production easier and more automatic, freeing millions of us to follow our bliss.

The Teacher Stays Home[7]

It is easy to point to changes in most jobs that have been brought about by technology. Manufacturers that once employed a thousand workers at a particular plant may now need no more than fifty to run the automated plant smoothly. Companies may now choose to use communication technologies to maintain good relations with clients in distant locations without opening branch offices.

Technology is changing things for workers as well. Telecommuting is growing in popularity in scattered parts of the country—in urban areas, for example, where commuting times seriously impact the quality of life. It wouldn't take much—a sharp increase in gasoline prices and some improvement in the speed of home connections, the current weakest link in the IP[8] (Internet Protocols) chain, for the number of telecommuters to increase dramatically.

Colleges, for their part, have built impressive campus networks, provided their students with e-mail accounts, and placed computers in faculty offices. However, it is clear that most universities see distributed learning courses and programs as secondary to their central mission of providing face-to-face instruction in brick and mortar classrooms. Likewise, community colleges are struggling to define their roles in bridging the digital divide without detracting from their well-established roles as learning centers for their communities.

While it's unlikely that employers will drive significant improvements to home access, there is growing interest among retailers and perhaps within the government, which may view interactivity as a tool to prop up interest in—and support for—the republic, in the possibilities. The foot race among the phone, cable, and satellite providers to bring high-speed access to the home is finally heating up as the market grows. The slow pace of their competition in the face of increasing consumer demand has mocked those who predicted that fast, two-way channels to homes were a prerequisite for entertainment and shopping. This revolution will be televised and we find ourselves in the curious position of waiting for demand to rise enough to trigger the deployment of technology which has existed for quite some time. Universal high-speed access will come eventually. When it does, education will be able to take advantage of the technology along with the entertainment industry.

But will education be ready for the change?

The Students Stay Home, Too—Some of Them

Imagine that it is 2010. Students at an urban community college are getting ready for their days. Some of them are groggy, having stayed up late the night before to do research for a class project using the statewide, online library collection. Others have risen earlier to catch up on e-mail (personal as well as professional; some of it even work-related), submit assignments, check on new assignments, review classmates' submissions, and post to ongoing discussions. Some of them finish their mail, grab a last cup of coffee, and head out the door for work.

What's going on here? Why will anyone physically go to work when we live in a digital global village?

One of the hardest things to grasp about the digital world is that much of it will look like our current world. Technologies to allow many of us to work from home—chiefly phone and fax—have been available for years. But, guess what? Many people like to go to work. The social environment is stimulating and pleasant. Even videophones (which are finally becoming affordable) won't replace the banter and camaraderie that offices—at their best—afford. Some of us will always prefer leaving home to go to work.

The same is true for school. Some learners are always going to prefer face-to-face interactions for some types of learning, even when we've made major improvements in our ability to represent ourselves in virtual space.[9]

Just as video rentals have not (altogether) replaced movie-going (and movie theaters have not entirely displaced stage plays), virtual learning will not soon—and perhaps never—replace face-to-face learning. If anything, the digital world mantra is "and/with" and not "either/or." It's about adding and multiplying choices, not about reducing them. So, think of virtual learning as a kind of drive-through: It won't replace indoor dining, but it will offer students another alternative.

How will colleges prepare for this explosion in customized learning, sometimes characterized as the shift from one-size-fits-all learning (mass-production
education) to just-in-time learning (episodic education) to just-for-me learning
(personalized instruction). Many ramifications result from this transition, and
increased cost is one of them.[10]

Story Problem

Many of us saw the gleam in the comptroller's eyes when she or he first heard
about virtual classrooms and virtual learning. Imagine a lecture hall as large as
the Internet itself! The seating capacity is infinite! Cost-per-unit of instruction
will fall off the chart.

The dream of an educational money machine in which ever-increasing tuition dollars offset the fixed costs of offering technology-mediated instruction
is a mirage. We won't get there. The scale-up costs are so enormous that by the
time they are recouped the game will have changed again.

Running a high-speed network in thirty- to fifty-year-old buildings is expensive. Period. New construction offers the best possibilities for installing an
adequate network at an affordable price. But how many K–12 districts, colleges,
or universities are in a building mode these days?

Beyond the wiring, you'll need routers and servers. Figure one server for
mail, one for file-sharing, one for the Web, one for back-up, one for a news group
or some other discussion forum; you begin to get the picture.

Each of these servers requires staff to support it. If you're going to run an
online program, you're going to need some sort of twenty-four-hour server support, as well as end-user support. Virtual students don't always work during so-
called normal business hours. Whether they want to or not, schools with virtual
learning programs become 24/7 institutions.

After the wiring come the nodes in the network—the computers, and they
don't come cheaply. Check for yourself.

- Choose a sound ratio of students to machines (assuming round-the-clock
  usage, say 24:1 giving students an hour per day; ignore most experts' recommendations to keep the ratio closer to 12:1).

- Choose a hardware/software package for approximately $1,200. That fig-
  ure might seem high in an age where $800 machines are advertised in Sun-
  day newspaper supplements. However, if you factor in training, support,
  and replacement costs (and you should), it is actually low.

- Determine the cost at your institution to provide a sufficient number of
  machines.

Then add about 50 percent of this figure to cover the cost of the network. Even if you already have a network and it's new this year, you'd better
begin budgeting to replace it. If it's more than a couple years old, it probably

isn't adequate anyway. Videoconferencing is hammering at your door, and it will consume seven times its weight in bandwidth faster than you can say "nanosecond."

No one has done a very good job of calculating the real staff costs for providing good support for the hardware, software, and users, but 150 percent of the network and computer costs isn't a bad estimate.

So what looked like a bargain—a classroom without walls and with no seating limit—turns out to be much more expensive (and tricky to manage) than a traditional classroom with tables and chairs.

Still, virtual classrooms offer some potential cost savings. Once strong networks are built and students routinely come to school with computers, schools may be able to concentrate on maintaining the infrastructure and let students worry about upgrading the machines to keep pace. This "dry county" model—where students' schools provide the set ups and students bring the kicker—remains elusive. The increasing sophistication of web-able cell phones and personal digital assistants and the falling costs of laptop and notebook computers give some hope for this scenario, as does the appearance of a variety of lower-cost "net stations" designed first and foremost to access network resources.

The savings come not from replacing existing classrooms but from using virtual classrooms to augment existing physical ones. The community colleges where I have taught have Byzantine space utilization problems. During prime class times, there may very well be no classrooms available, allowing zero capacity for growth. At other times, classes run very small, if they run at all.

Thus, some schools find themselves acquiring additional classroom space to meet demand for only a few hours a day—hardly a bargain. Virtual classrooms, because of their inherent round-the-clock accessibility, are much more cost effective in exactly the type of environment schools face today.

My dream for a school in 2010 is a sharp departure from today's patterns. Instead of students coming to class five days a week, or three days a week, or two days a week to attend a class, students would come to school one day a week and attend all their classes. They would meet their teachers, work with their study groups, visit the library for research, and do the activities for which face-to-face interaction is best suited. During the rest of the week, they would use virtual classrooms and virtual learning resources to do their work.

My current school is already contemplating alternatives to meet increased demand for classrooms and parking in the popular morning, early afternoon, and evening hours. What if the school could meet this demand not by adding building square footage or paving more grass, but by drastically changing the patterns by which students and teachers come to school?

A one-day-a-week schedule quintuples the capacity of classrooms and parking lots, and this assumes we adhere to a five-day schedule—the gains are greater if we add Saturday and Sunday, which many schools already do. Schools aren't even close to being the first to schedule over a longer week: For years, some large manufacturers have run essentially dual work forces to meet increased demand for a product and adjust to employee absenteeism on Fridays and Mondays. Some workers work weekdays, others work a weekend shift with perhaps a Friday or a Monday tacked on.

We have become used to the idea that the information revolution represents a paradigm shift, but our habituation causes us to lose sight of the scale of this transformation. We are not living through an incremental change (though many of the changes that touch us most nearly proceed rather slowly — the morphing of our television into our computer, for example), but through one that will alter most of the patterns of our life.

Where Politics Comes In

We have already discussed the critical issue of access in our information revolution. It may not be overstating the case to say that access to technology is as important to this revolution as freedom was to the American and French revolutions.

The demographics of the Internet in its current manifestation (essentially the Web and e-mail) are instructive — and a bit chilling.[11] O'Reilly and Associates (1995) found that nearly half (48 percent) of U.S. households with Internet Service reported annual incomes of at least $50,000. The 10th WWW User Survey (1998), prepared by Graphics, Visualization and Useability Center at the Georgia Institute of Technology, reported similar results. While it is difficult to establish numbers for comparison, the O'Reilly numbers, if accurate, suggest that higher-income groups are disproportionately represented among homes with Internet access.

Part of the Dystopia view of the digital world is that it widens the chasm between the haves and the have-nots. Like it or not, digital technologies could be instrumental in creating an underclass that is forever blocked from enjoying the benefits of the society because they are denied the means (tools and knowledge) to access those benefits. It is imperative that schools resist this tendency.

Community colleges have long played a critical role in providing access to higher education. Much of the nation's population lives within a few miles of a community-college campus, and in 1997, 5.3 million U.S. citizens attended 1,200 community colleges.[12] Because of this tradition and because of the initiative community colleges have shown in bringing innovative courses and programs to widely varied audiences by way of distance learning technologies,[13] it is reasonable to expect that community colleges will continue to play a key role in fostering access to higher education.

The second, highly political aspect arising from the integration of information technologies into community-college classrooms is that these technologies radically reshape the role of the teacher and the nature of his or her work.

Despite a great deal of talk to the contrary, the lecture is still the premier instructional technique in college classrooms, even at community colleges. Just walk around your campus during the first week of classes. In most rooms, you'll hear the sound of one voice talking. Information technology makes that technique problematic.

Materials presented by the teacher (on Web pages, in e-mail messages, or in conference postings) can be quickly and easily compared to other information, which, after all, is only a mouse click away. Even when students aren't explicitly instructed to look for comparisons, my experience suggests that they often make this discovery for themselves. When was the last time a student at your college went to the library to research a topic presented in a lecture?

This shift in emphasis need not be a bad thing. From my perspective, one of the best things about technology-mediated learning is its tendency to call into question some of our fundamental assumptions about learning. Rethinking these assumptions produces valuable insights about specific learning objectives and the best way to attain them. The best assignments are technology-independent. That is, they work well in conventional classrooms as well as virtual ones, via voice as well as via e-mail.

The integration of information technologies also produces significant changes in the working conditions. Because community-college faculty members are slightly more likely than four-year university faculty to work under the terms of a bargained labor agreement, these changes will substantially impact collective bargaining over the next ten to fifteen years.

Traditional definitions of workday and work week—even the definitions of class time, class size, and load—evaporate in the mnemonic light of the virtual classroom. Students in face-to-face classrooms are accustomed to waiting until the next class period to ask questions about course materials. Students in virtual classrooms can ask questions instantly. Even half a day seems like an eternity in an environment where time is measured in thousandths of a second.

The distinction between weekdays and weekends also is difficult to sustain. Especially as more and more students choose technology-mediated schooling to make room for college in their overfull lives, weekends become prime time for schoolwork. Contemporary learning theory is much engaged in the postmodern equivalent of a grail quest: the search to define the "teachable moment" for a variety of students in a variety of disciplines.[14]

Is it possible to address the full range of teachable moments for students in technology-mediated classes if we start by excluding nearly 30 percent of a week? The list of changes resulting from integrating technology into an educational system goes on and on. One of the most important shifts, the movement away from an instructor-centered classroom and toward a learner-centered classroom, deserves special consideration.

While it is certain that different disciplines will experience the effects of technology differently, it is also likely that there will turn out to be a great deal of similarity across disciplines. Because I am chiefly a writing teacher, my emphasis will be on the writing classroom.

The Wired Writing Classroom

Earlier in this chapter I mentioned some of the collateral results of moving from an actual classroom to a virtual one. In this section, I'd like to review the shifts mentioned previously and expand on them.

The shift away from an educational model that places the instructor at the center and views her or him as the focus of learning began long before the computer appeared on our societal horizon, but wired classrooms amplify and hasten this shift in predictable ways, and in some surprising ways as well.

Background levels of information are much higher in wired classrooms than in conventional ones. In addition to all the knowledge and experience students bring with them to class, access to great stores of information are but a few keystrokes away, hastening the shift from teacher-as-sage to teacher-as-guide. Students need teachers to help them learn to navigate these webs of information, to gain experience in evaluating sources and analyzing the information they contain, and to become proficient in weaving links into their own documents. There will be less and less need for teachers to dispense information.

Apart from these changes in the context of learning, the Information Age is also producing changes in the *lingua franca* of the classroom. Students and teachers have always, to some extent, brought differing languages with them to the classroom. Wired classrooms emphasize and even exaggerate the differences among these languages.

Take the concept of a *page*. For most teachers today, the page is a clear, well-defined entity. After all, we know it from reading thousands (perhaps even hundreds of thousands) of pages during our careers. Our students—many of whom have substantially less reading experience to begin with—have a notion of page that is also shaped to a large degree by their experiences with e-mail, newsgroups, and the Web. It is not too far-fetched to claim that their concept of *screen* may be as powerful as our concept of page.[15]

In addition to influencing teachers' roles and creating new ways of designating units of text, the digital revolution is also accelerating our era's movement toward greater informality in writing. In some ways, digital texts are closer to speech than to writing. They have a similar ad hoc quality that invites us to leave our dress clothes in the closet and go casual. The temptation to irreverence is sometimes irresistible, a tendency you may have noticed in this article. Wired classrooms emphasize this informality and irreverence.

The Information Age exerts many other influences on the classroom and, like the others we have mentioned, these influences are exaggerated by the wired classroom. New words spring up regularly (many Web sites post neologisms as a kind of public service) and new usages spring up around new ways of behaving. These influences are already familiar to us: New technologies always bring new vocabularies to living languages.[16] Other influences, while perhaps less easy to see, may have longer-reaching consequences.

When all communication—telephone, fax, e-mail, Web access, live chat, videoconferencing—is billed by bandwidth rather than by connection time, conciseness will become an even greater virtue.[17] True, words take up very little bandwidth compared to video, but the more concise the text, the more bandwidth can be devoted to color, pictures, and even moving pictures. Economy of language will take on additional layers of meaning.

Attention as Currency

In *Wired* magazine, Michael Goldhaber (1997) suggested that, in the brave new digital world, attention may replace money as our primary means of exchange.[18] As farfetched as that idea may seem to us at the moment, it really is possible to imagine a world where corporations would not pay a broadcasting company $1.11 million for 30 seconds of Super Bowl advertising, because there could never be an audience large enough to justify the expense. If we have 125 channels (already available in some areas) or 250 or 500 or 1,000 or even 1 million channels (possible but hardly conceivable), what we will watch? How many of us will watch the same things?

It will be many years (centuries, perhaps, if history is any indication) before we come to terms with the changes made to our societies and ourselves by the digital revolution. Within the technology exists both the possibility to further isolate us from each other (and to estrange us from ourselves) and the hope for greater connection among people throughout the world.

Is the electronic global village a Balkan reality? Or is it a virtual nirvana?

I believe that our ultimate response to those questions will depend on our first finding reasonable answers to questions regarding access. Community colleges can play an important role in finding those answers. Composition classes, because they are well-suited to wired classrooms and because of their status as required courses in most curricula, are a good place for community colleges to begin their efforts.

Notes

1. Surely the symphony of headlines has sufficiently heralded its arrival. If not, Michael G. Dolence decreed its arrival in his keynote presentation to the Continuous Quality Improvement Network (CQIN) Summer Institute in July 1997. See his homepage at (http://www.mgdolence.com/) for more details.

2. *Wired Tools,* 5.12 (December 1997).

3. I am using *society* in the sense of its third definition in the *American Heritage CD Dictionary* (1997). "The institutions and culture of a distinct self-perpetuating group."

4. That is, schools are where we learn the rules, guidelines, and conventions for the society in which we live. Language is the primary medium for this transmission. There have always been tensions within this role for schools. Families, neighborhoods, churches, and, increasingly as we enter the twentieth-first century, mass media also transmit and replicate culture in succeeding generations.

5. http://www.slip.net/~spage/gibson/biblio.htm for a close-up look at this world.

6. See A. Rogers, "Global Literacy in a Gutenberg Culture," (http://www.gsn.bilkent.edu.tr/teach/articles/gutenberg.html) for a discussion of the origins of this phrase in the work of Marshall McLuhan.

7. This heading pays homage to Donald Murray, with a nod to Peter Elbow for good measure.

8. Internet Protocols are the common set of rules and standards that allow machines made by different manufacturers and running different operating systems to communicate with each other on the Internet.

9. In all but the most sophisticated (read "expensive") environments, users are represented textually (names, nicknames) and occasionally by symbols or simple, cartoon avatars. Three dimensional avatars are still the stuff of science-fiction novels.

10. http://www.microsoft.com.

11. http://www.ora.com/research/users/results.html

12. http://www.ed.gov/offices/OVAE/CCLO/edreform.html

13. The wealth of audio courses, telecourses, satellite courses, and interactive television courses, all of which predate courses via e-mail or the Web, offered by community colleges nationwide is clear testament to their success in this area.

14. As nearly as I can determine, Rosalia Hamilton, a participant in the Raritan Valley Community College's "Ethics, Values and Technology Project" (funded by the National Science Foundation) coined this expression to describe the teaching strategy the project was defining. Hamilton's "teachable moment" is similar in some respects to Vygotsky's "zone of proximal development."

15. I have noticed something like this at work in students' responses to my e-mail and postings in discussion areas. What I find sufficient and adequate they often find wordy and overkill. I believe part of the difference is that my postings frequently exceed a screen's worth of writing—I'm still reaching toward the page.

16. Even to French, despite the best efforts of the Academy.

17. This is one of those predictions about which I'm quite certain but for which I wouldn't want to name a date.

18. "Attention Shoppers!" *Wired* 5.12. (December 1997) (http://www.wired.com/wired/5.12/es_attention.html).

Works Cited

10th WWW User Survey. 1998. Graphics, Visualization and Useability Center, Georgia Institute of Technology. (http://www.gvu.gatech.edu/user_surveys/survey-1998-10/). Last accessed, November 2000.

"Community College Education Reform Practices: For All American Students." Community College Liaison Office, Office of Adult and Vocational Education, United States Department of Education. (http://www.ed.gov/offices/OVAE/CCLO/edreform.html). Last accessed, November 2000.

Dolence, M. "The Dawn of the Information Age." (http://www.mgdolence.com/) Last accessed, November 2000.

Dyson. E. 1997. *Release2*. New York: Broadway Books.

Elbow, P. 1973. *Writing Without Teachers.* New York: Oxford University Press.

———. Spring–Summer 1990. "Forward: About Personal Expressive Academic Writing." *Pre-Text. A Journal of Rhetorical Theory* 11(1–2): 7–20.

Goldhaber, M. H. "Attention Shoppers!" *Wired* 5.12 (http://www.wired.com/wired/5.12/es_attention.html). Last accessed, November 2000.

Herring, S. C., ed. 1996. *Computer-Mediated Communication: Linguistic, Social, and Cross-Cultural Perspectives.* Amsterdam: John Benjamins.

Internet User Survey. 1995. O'Reilly & Associates. (http://www.ora.com/research/users/results.html). Last accessed, November 2000.

Negroponte, N. 1995. *Being Digital.* New York: Knopf.

Mander, J. 1991. *In the Absence of the Sacred.* San Francisco: Sierra Club Books.

———. 1977. *Four Arguments for the Elimination of Television.* New York: William Morrow.

Mitchell, W. J. 1995. *City of Bits: Space, Place, and the Infobahn.* Cambridge: MIT P.

Murray, D. 1985. *A Writer Teaches Writing.* New York: Houghton Mifflin.

———. 1991. "One Writer's Curriculum." *English Journal.* 80(4)(April): 16–20.

Postman, N. 1993. *Technopoly.* New York: Vintage Books.

Rogers, A. "Global Literacy in a Gutenberg Culture." (http://www.gsn.bilkent.edu.tr/teach/articles/gutenberg.html). Last accessed, November 2000.

Scaff, J. 1995. "Architecting Cyberspace: The Poetry & Paradox of Liquid Environments." *Issues in Electronic Culture.* (November 30) (http://pixels.filmtv.ucla.edu/courses/courses95-96/issues_f95/julian_scaff/paper.html). Last accessed, November 2000.

Sproull, L., & S. Kiesler. 1989. *Connections: New Ways of Working in the Networked Organization.* Cambridge: MIT P.

Turkle, S. 1995. *Life on the Screen: Identity in the Age of the Internet.* New York: Simon & Schuster.

Zuboff, S. 1988. *In the Age of the Smart Machine.* New York. Basic Books.

Afterword

The Community College: Still Cooling Out
Ira Shor

Like a postmodern ancient mariner, I have multiple albatrosses hanging from my neck. One of these abused birds is the community college—To be honest about the two-year college albatross, I'd have to report that I was raised to be a working-class snob. I was taught to look down on neighborhood peers who could do no better than attend a community college. My path took me from lousy schools in the working-class South Bronx to the magisterial Bronx High School of Science in the far-away, fashionable northwest of the borough I grew up in. From there, I went on to two elite universities and met transfer students from community colleges to whom I felt superior. Imagine my humbling surprise when, as a new Ph.D. in the summer of 1971, I was hired by a community college, only to go there and find that this strange institution had so much to teach me and changed my life; my work; and my way of seeing, learning, and teaching.

Back then, I was a newly minted, unemployed literature Ph.D., unable to land a job despite my fancy doctorate, sleeping on my parent's living-room sofa, too old for such a thing, really. My bookkeeper mom had dreamed of having educated sons who went to the colleges closed to her in her Shakespeare-loving Depression youth; my working-class dad who had dropped out of school at fifteen and now wondered if my twenty-one years of schooling were worth it, so much education and so little to show. He pounded steel for a living, a bulky and bawdy graduate of "the School of Hard Knocks," as he put it. I had dwindling cash and a red VW bug, just enough money and wheels to make it cross-country to California, the golden land, where I planned to make a life somehow. Just as I was about to head west, a last-minute call came from the English Department at Staten Island Community College. They wanted me to teach remedial writing in the open-admissions program then underway on campuses of the troubled City University of New York. Suddenly, I became an assistant professor who could stop sleeping on sofas. I was employed! A real grownup at last! My first day on campus, I felt like kissing the concrete quadrangle that brought me a paycheck ($820 for that September of 1971). I had no idea where this paycheck and concrete would take me in the coming decades. This place made me into a kind of teacher and writer I never imagined becoming. I learned what literacy and social class meant. I gained respect for the dedicated teachers and resilient students who inhabit these grossly underfunded sites of mass higher education.

My respect for the teachers and students of working-class campuses was renewed when I read the disturbing essays included in this book. The intelligent studies here bluntly and hopefully question what we do and where we do it when we act as writing teachers at community colleges. They have helped me rethink my own three-decade effort to deploy a critical-democratic pedagogy in my literacy classes at a working-class campus on Staten Island. These bustling sites of student hope and teacher devotion are too invisible, misrepresented, and dismissed. Take, for example, a new taxonomy of colleges proposed by Robert Zemsky and William Massy of Stanford, reported favorably by Chester Finn (1998), a former Reagan-Bush official. In this scheme, community colleges are unapologetically described as "convenience institutions" dispensing "user-friendly" drive-in training, not to be confused with the serious learning underway at "brand-name" places like Berkeley and Duke. Forever at the bottom of the status and funding hierarchies, community colleges "don't get no respect", as Rodney Dangerfield has been heard to say. The need is obvious to raise the profile of community colleges and the enormous writing enterprise underway there, the invisible "other" of academe. The meager representation of community colleges in composition and rhetoric journals and books further characterizes the invisibility of these discriminated campuses. This book helps correct the unbalanced and inadequate discourse surrounding the two-year campuses.

Perhaps Finn, a sometime Fellow at the conservative Hudson Institute, finds community colleges "convenient" because he never has to deal with them or with the students who never get to elegant brand-name places, like Vanderbilt, where Finn has taught. Actually, my working-class students find college not so convenient when they have to juggle jobs and families with passing courses, doing homework, and paying rising tuition costs. They lack the elite luxuries of free time and plentiful income that helps students grow into intellectual life. Treated as people who don't count, they can be dismissed by Finn and others as "drive-in" customers in the learning malls of America. In an unequal society, it seems that schools, colleges, and teachers count only if their students count. Further, students count only if they pay high tuition and come from upper-income homes (the most important indicator of college retention and success). Visibility and status to accompany high tuition and the lushness of your academic address. Teachers or students whose academic address is a community college have a hard time being taken seriously in academe as well as in the political media and professional worlds.

Perhaps the political dilemma here is obvious and the rhetorical question is begging: Do low-tuition, open-access community colleges democratize higher education or do they represent an antidemocratic segregation of working-class students onto subordinate campuses with lesser funding, vocationalized curricula, poorer facilities, and fewer services? This question is the eight-hundred-pound gorilla that can't fit into any closet. It's in the middle of the room waiting to be dealt with. Books like this one keep visible the gorilla issue of equity, which is the primary problem in teaching at community colleges. Because literacy and learning are historical and context-bound, as Scribner and Cole (1981), Graff (1987), and others have asserted, the unequal situation of the community-college student and teacher is the key starting point for designing and evaluating learning and pedagogy.

About inequality as the key issue, consider observations made by Kevin Dougherty (1991; 1994), whose astute work culminates a line of thought developed by Karabel (1972), Brint and Karabel (1989), Pincus (1980), and Pincus and Archer (1989), Zwerling (1976), and others:

> Entering a community college seriously hampers the educational success of baccalaureate aspirants, apart from any effect that results from community college students having, on average, lower test scores and aspirations than comparable four-year college entrants. This negative institutional effect is particularly distressing since the community college has become the main gateway into higher education for minority and working class students. (Dougherty 1991, 312)

Dougherty was updating and deepening our understanding of the "cooling out function" of community colleges first identified by Burton Clark in the late 1950s, whose descriptions of students being eased downward and outward also pointed to an "institutional" function of depressing aspirations. Dougherty concludes that

> . . . the fact that a greater proportion of community college students comes from disadvantaged backgrounds than four-year college students only partly explains their disparity in educational attainment. This gap is not attributable to student characteristics alone; it arises as well from the nature of the institution they are entering. Even when we restrict our analysis to baccalaureate aspirants of similar background and ability, those entering two-year colleges are significantly less likely to attain the bachelor's degree. (1991, 314)

Dougherty admits that "this is a difficult finding to accept." It is difficult because the community college has been bathed in official democratic rhetoric as a means that allows folks to overcome class and race distinctions. However, Clark, forty years ago, and Dougherty, in the 1990s, have told a different story. Similarly Cohen and Brawer put it this way in their history of the two-year system:

> Community colleges certainly performed an essential service in the 1960s and 1970s when a mass of people demanded access . . . How many universities would have been shattered if community colleges to which the petitioners could be shunted had not been available? (1982, 27)

Shunting is consistent with maintaining inequality but not with promoting democracy.

Would a society dominated by white, male, and corporate supremacy build 1,200 new community colleges to disturb its old hierarchies of race, gender, and class? Would an unequal system dismantle itself by distributing so many instruments for equality? If democracy and equality were in fact the goals of this postwar higher-education policy, why not simply expand existing four-year institutions and enroll all students on the same campuses with access to the same curricula, resources, and baccalaureate (the degree that counts in the job market)? Consider that in the heyday of community-college construction, the 1960s, a new two-year campus opened on the average of one every ten days for ten years. From 400,000 working students in 1959, these special campuses enrolled 4,000,000 by 1971, even more today. This is an enormous enterprise called into being by a status quo whose policies quarantined working students rather than equalized them. As the late Paulo Freire (Shor and Freire 1987) said, a system doesn't build schools and colleges to undermine itself, even though there is always space in education to act against the status quo and against unequal power and privilege, as the essays in this book show.

Inside community colleges, many teachers and students work against the shunting inequality these campuses represent, seeking human development, career advancement, and social justice, instead. This is what this book celebrates — not the community-college system itself — but the clever teachers and students inside who do what is possible to overcome institutional obstacles to critical learning. Democracy and equality are still down the road. Let's get there.

Works Cited

Brint, S., & Karabel, J. 1989. *The Diverted Dream.* New York: Oxford UP.

Cohen, A. M., & Brawer, F. 1982. *The American Community College.* San Francisco: Jossey-Bass.

Clark, B. 1960. "The Cooling Out Function in Higher Education." *American Journal of Sociology* 65 (May): 569–76.

———. 1980. "The 'Cooling Out' Function Revisited." In *Questioning the Community College Role: New Directions for Community Colleges,* No. 32, ed. G. Vaughan, 15–32. San Francisco: Jossey-Bass.

Dougherty, K. J. 1991. "The Community College at the Crossroads: The Need for Structural Reform." *Harvard Educational Review* 61 (August): 311–36.

———. 1994. *The Contradictory College.: The Conflicting Origins, Impacts, and Futures of the Community College.* Albany: SUNY P.

Finn, C. E., Jr. 1990. "Today's Academic Market Requires a New Taxonomy of Colleges." *The Chronicle of Higher Education* (January 9): 8 64–65.

Graff, H. J. 1987. *The Labyrinths of Literacy.* London: Falmeir Press.

Karabel, J. 1972. "Community Colleges and Social Stratification." *Harvard Educational Review.* 42 (August): 521–62.

Pincus, F. L. 1980. "The False Promises of Community Colleges." *Harvard Educational Review* 50 (August): 332–61.

Pincus, F. L., & Archer, E. 1989. *Bridges to Opportunity? Are Community Colleges Meeting the Transfer Needs of Minority Students?* New York: The College Board.

Scribner, S., & Cole, M. 1981. *The Psychology of Literacy.* Cambridge: Harvard UP.

Shor, I. 1980/1987. *Critical Teaching and Everyday Life.* Chicago: U of Chicago P.

Shor, I., & P. Freire. 1987. *A Pedagogy for Liberation: Dialogues on Transforming Education.* Milford, CT: Greenwood Press.

Zwerling, L. S. 1976. *Second Best: The Crisis of the Junior College.* New York: McGraw-Hill.